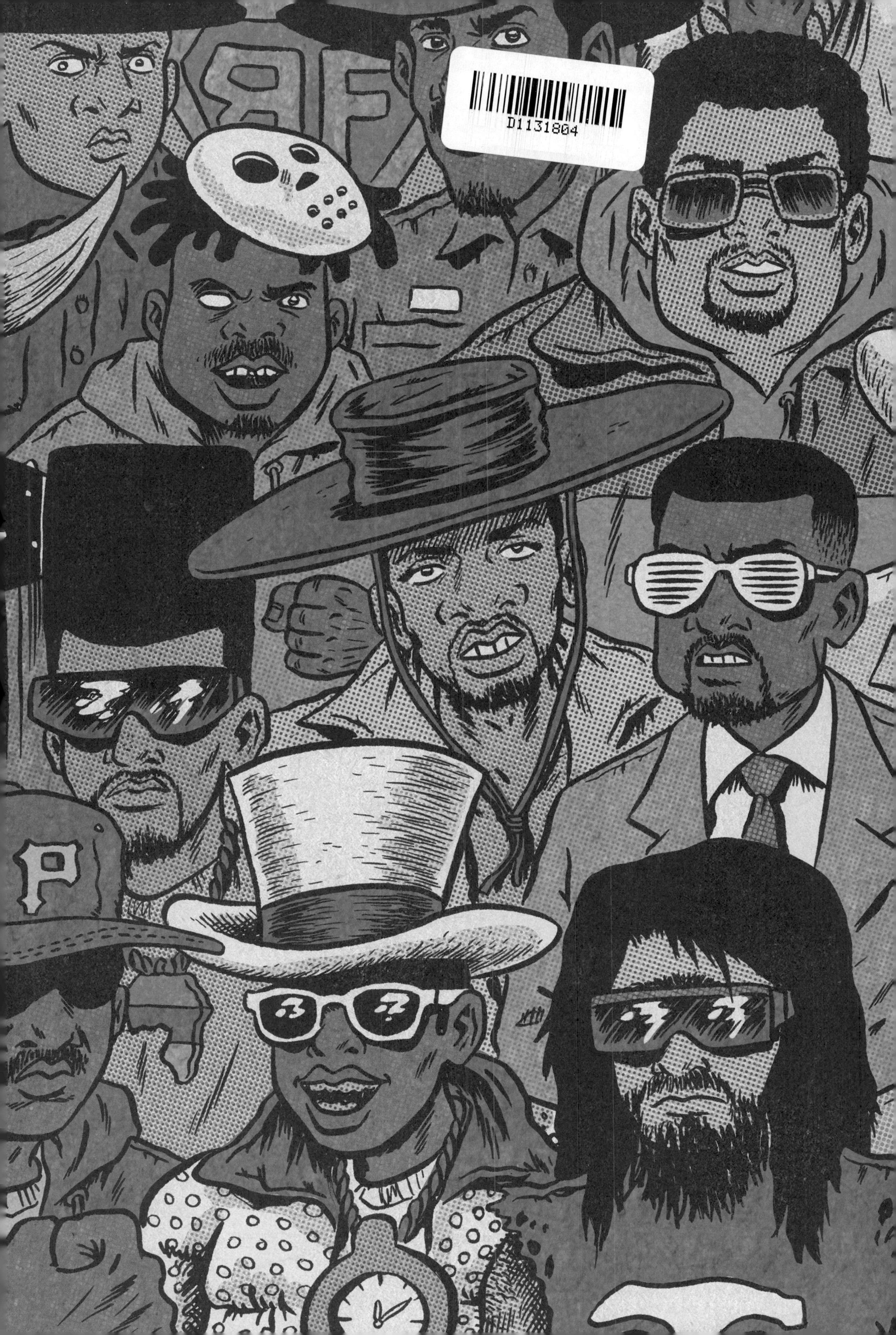

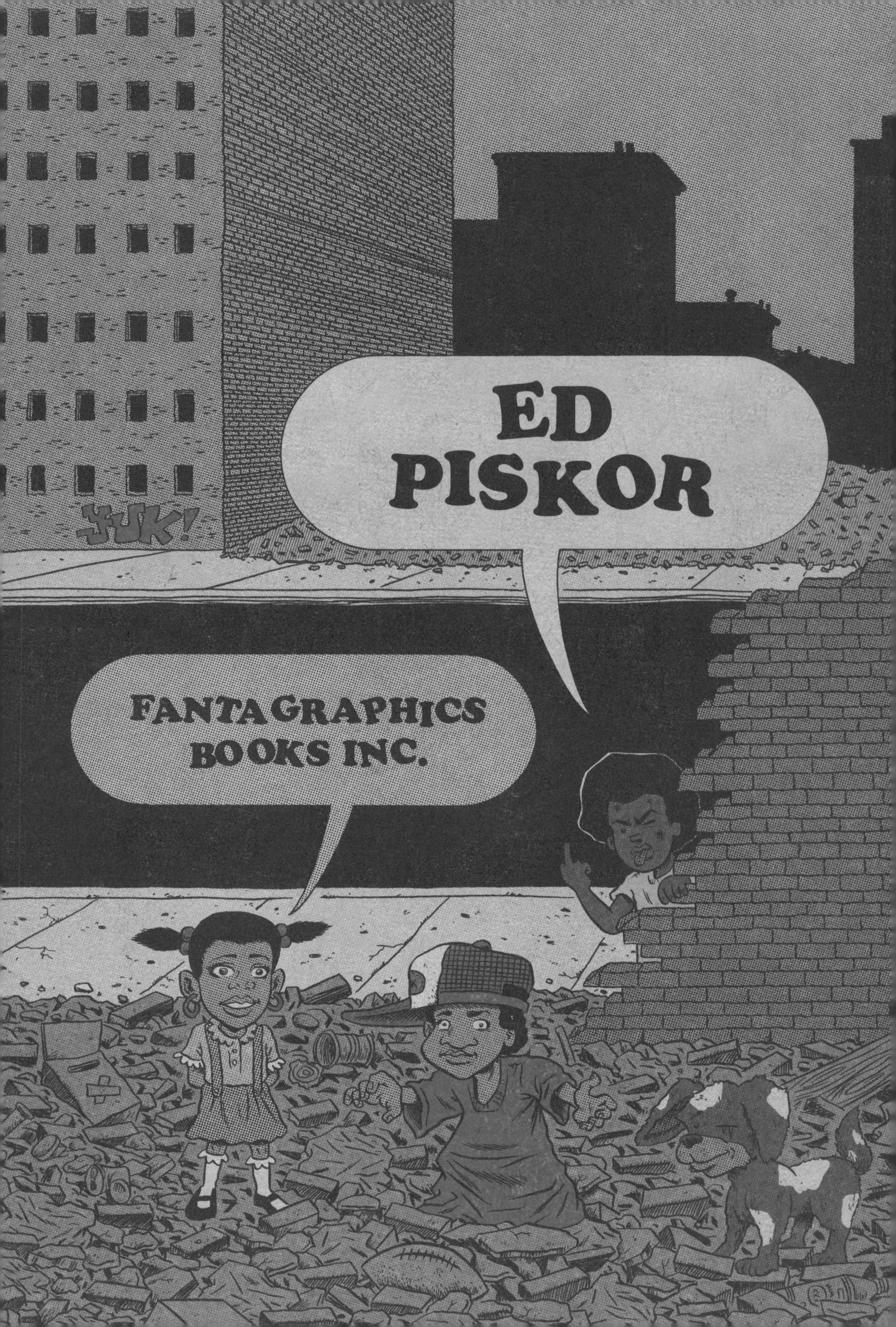
ED PISKOR
FANTAGRAPHICS BOOKS INC.

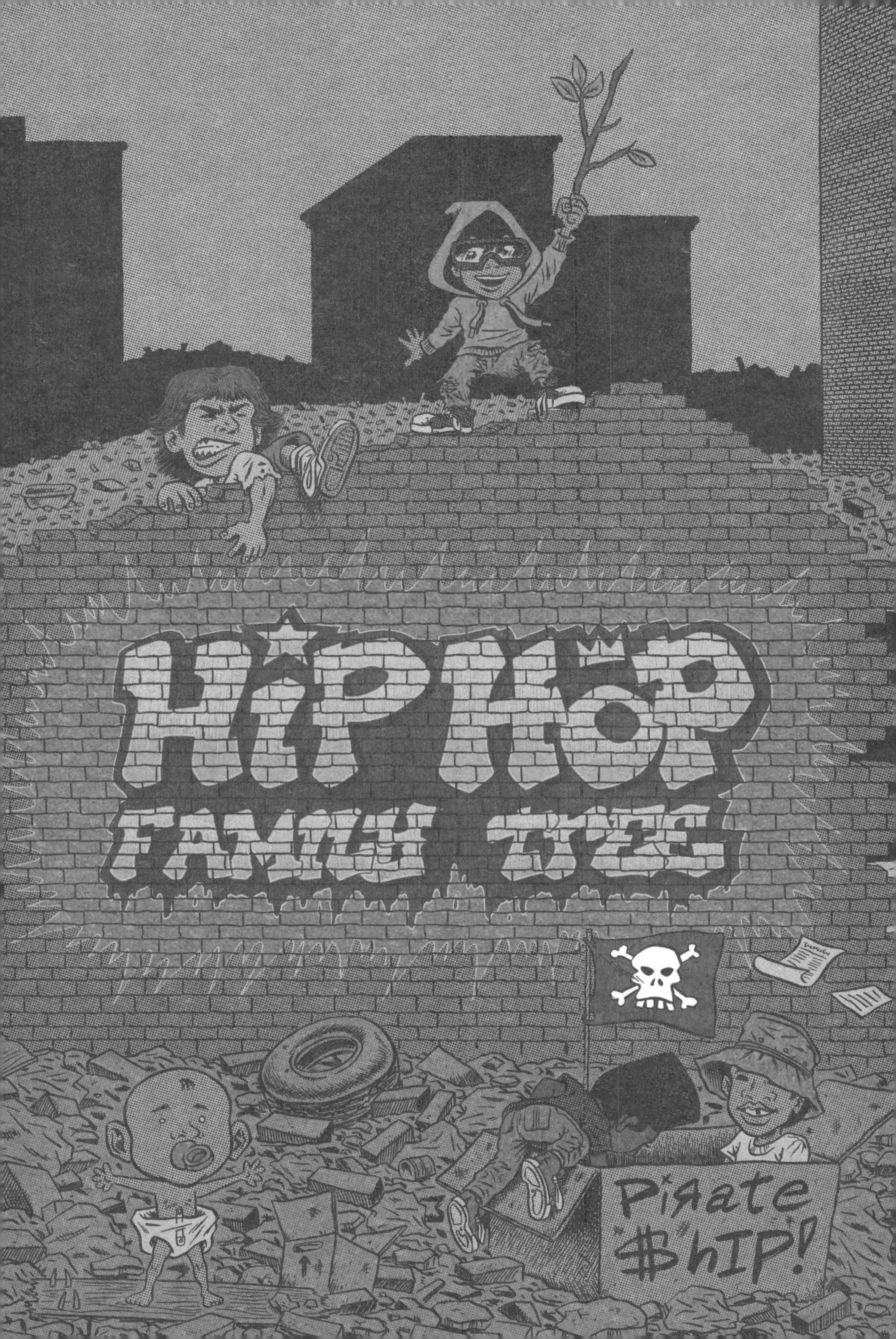
HIP HOP
FAMILY TREE
PiRate $hIP!

ROGUES GALLERY

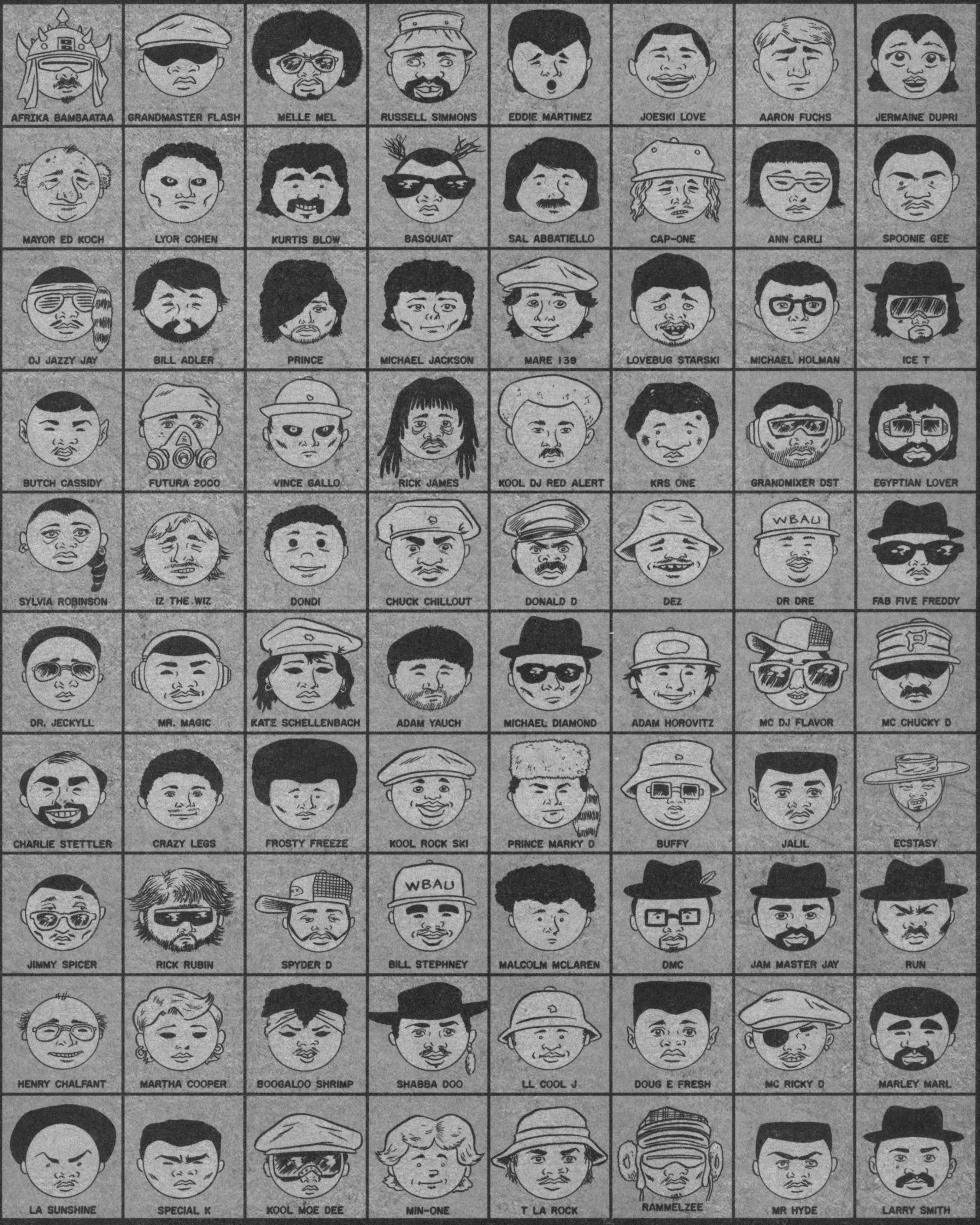
AFRIKA BAMBAATAA
GRANDMASTER FLASH
MELLE MEL
RUSSELL SIMMONS
EDDIE MARTINEZ
JOESKI LOVE
AARON FUCHS
JERMAINE DUPRI
MAYOR ED KOCH
LYOR COHEN
KURTIS BLOW
BASQUIAT
SAL ABBATIELLO
CAP-ONE
ANN CARLI
SPOONIE GEE
DJ JAZZY JAY
BILL ADLER
PRINCE
MICHAEL JACKSON
MARE 139
LOVEBUG STARSKI
MICHAEL HOLMAN
ICE T
BUTCH CASSIDY
FUTURA 2000
VINCE GALLO
RICK JAMES
KOOL DJ RED ALERT
KRS ONE
GRANDMIXER DST
EGYPTIAN LOVER
SYLVIA ROBINSON
IZ THE WIZ
DONDI
CHUCK CHILLOUT
DONALD D
DEZ
WBAU
DR DRE
FAB FIVE FREDDY
DR. JECKYLL
MR. MAGIC
KATE SCHELLENBACH
ADAM YAUCH
MICHAEL DIAMOND
ADAM HOROVITZ
MC DJ FLAVOR
MC CHUCKY D
CHARLIE STETTLER
CRAZY LEGS
FROSTY FREEZE
KOOL ROCK SKI
PRINCE MARKY D
BUFFY
JALIL
ECSTASY
JIMMY SPICER
RICK RUBIN
SPYDER D
WBAU
BILL STEPHNEY
MALCOLM MCLAREN
DMC
JAM MASTER JAY
RUN
HENRY CHALFANT
MARTHA COOPER
BOOGALOO SHRIMP
SHABBA DOO
LL COOL J
DOUG E FRESH
MC RICKY D
MARLEY MARL
LA SUNSHINE
SPECIAL K
KOOL MOE DEE
MIN-ONE
T LA ROCK
RAMMELZEE
MR HYDE
LARRY SMITH

HiP HoP
FAMILY TREE

TABLE OF CONTENTS

I DEDICATE THIS TO YOU FOR BELIEVING IN ME.

FANTAGRAPHICS BOOKS

7563 LAKE CITY WAY, NE
SEATTLE, WASHINGTON 98115

EDITORIAL LIASON: GARY GROTH
PRODUCTION: PAUL BARESH
PUBLISHER: GARY GROTH
ASSOCIATE PUBLISHER: ERIC REYNOLDS

FIRST FANTAGRAPHICS BOOKS EDITION: AUGUST 2015

ISBN: 978-1-60699-848-9   LIBRARY OF CONGRESS CONTROL NUMBER: 2015935149

PRINTED IN CHINA

INSPIRED BY WATCHING B-BOYS LIKE THE **ROCKSTEADY CREW** AT THE **ROXY**, THE **BEASTIE BOYS** DECIDE THAT IF THEY'RE GONNA KEEP DOING **COVERS** TO THEIR FAVORITE RAP SONGS, THEN THEY SHOULD LOOK AND ACT THE PART ON STAGE. THIS INCLUDES CREATING NAMES THAT THEY CAN **IRON-ON** TO THEIR **CARVEL ICE CREAM** SHIRTS.

ADAM YAUCH	ADAM HOROVITZ	MICHAEL DIAMOND	KATE SCHELLENBACH

THE BEASTIES' PAL, **RICK RUBIN**, IS SIMPATICO IN THAT HIS LIFE ALSO IS BEING TAKEN OVER BY **HIP HOP**.

SORRY, BUT GIRLS DON'T SOUND GOOD AT **RAPPING**. NOT AT ALL.

KATE

KEEP IN MIND THAT RICK AND THE GROUP **STILL** FREQUENT **PUNK ROCK** CLUBS. THAT'S THE MAGIC ABOUT THIS MOMENT OF TIME IN **NYC**...

THE KING ADROCK

...BECAUSE ON THE **SAME** NIGHT, THEY CAN **ALSO** CATCH DJS LIKE **AFRIKA BAMBAATAA** AND **JAZZY JAY** AT PLACES LIKE **NEGRIL**.

THE **BEASTIES** DON'T COMPLAIN THAT **RICK RUBIN** FOOTS THE BILL FOR ALL THE **SHENANIGANS**.

MENUDO!

HA HA!

HAW!

THIS JUST FEELS **RIGHT**.

5

KATE SCHELLENBACH, THE BEASTIE BOYS DRUMMER, ISN'T SUPPOSED TO BE IN TOWN RIGHT NOW.

HI, KATE...

...UM, RICK THINKS WE GOT A GOOD SHOT AT BEING THE FIRST WHITE RAP GROUP.

THE CORE GROUP, ALONG WITH KATE, STILL PLAY HARDCORE MUSIC SOMETIMES UNDER THE NAME YOUNG AND THE USELESS. THE ALL-MALE BEASTIE BOYS HAVE ACTUALLY STARTED WRITING THEIR OWN RHYMES TO PERFORM ON STAGE TO SUPPLEMENT THEIR RAP MUSIC COVERS AND NONSENSE.

MCA

EVERYBODY IN THE WORLD...

ADROCK

...WHOEVER YOU ARE...

MIKE D

...YOU BETTER GET READY...

DJ DOUBLE R!!

RICK RUBIN ISN'T MUCH OF A DJ IN THE SPIRIT OF HIP HOP, BUT HE HAS ALL THE BEST EQUIPMENT, HE LOOKS GOOD BEHIND THE BEASTIES AND HE ACTS LIKE HE KNOWS WHAT HE'S DOING.

IN THE LATE '70S, **MARTHA COOPER** HAD BEEN A STAFF PHOTOGRAPHER FOR THE **NEW YORK POST** FOR YEARS.

SNAP!

IN HER SPARE TIME SHE'D WORK ON A PASSION PROJECT SHE CALLS "STREET PLAY."

I CALL 'ER **PIDGEY**...

TAKING PHOTOS OF KIDS AMUSING THEMSELVES WITHOUT PARENTAL SUPERVISION BRINGS HER ALL OVER NEW YORK'S URBAN SPRAWL.

WHY NOT TAKE FLICKS OF GRAFFITI ARTISTS, **MISS MARTHA**?

GOOD QUESTION, **HE-3**.

WANNA MEET A KING?

SNAP

THE "**KING**" INTRODUCED TO MARTHA IS NONE OTHER THAN GRAFFITI LEGEND **DONDI WHITE**.

YOU TOOK A FLICK OF MY WORK IN THE PAPER A WHILE AGO. IT'S IN MY SCRAPBOOK. THANKS.

DONDI, YOU'LL REMEMBER, HELPED WITH THE FILMING OF **WILD STYLE**.*

* HHFT BOOK 2 -- EAZY ED

MARTHA AND **DONDI** BECOME FAST FRIENDS AND AN **UNPRECEDENTED** LEVEL OF **TRUST** DEVELOPS WHICH GAINS HER ACCESS INTO THIS SECRET WORLD OF **TRAINYARDS** AND **SPRAY PAINT**.

HENRY CHALFANT HAS BEEN WATCHING "GRAFF" DEVELOP FOR YEARS. HIS ARTISTIC MEDIUM IS **SCULPTURE**, BUT HE HAS A **CAMERA** AND HE DOCUMENTS WHAT HE SEES.

WOW!

HMM?

FOR SOME REASON IT TOOK HENRY FOREVER TO MEET **ANYONE** IN THE GRAFFITI WORLD.

THINK HE'S AN **UNDERCOVER PIG**?

SNAP

MAYBE HE WANNA TOUCH ON YUH **DICK** OR SOME'.

SKEME

WHEN WORD DOES GET OUT ABOUT HENRY HIS STUDIO BECOMES A HAVEN FOR GRAFFITI WRITERS.

HENRY, THIS IS LIKE A MASTERPIECE AWT GALLERY...

EVENTUALLY, CHALFANT BUILDS ENOUGH OF A BODY OF WORK THAT HE PROMOTES AN ART SHOW TO DISPLAY HIS PICS.

THIS IS WHERE **HENRY** AND **MARTHA** MEET.

CHEERS!

TINK

ON CALL ONE DAY, MARTHA IS **ORDERED** TO RUSH AND TAKE PHOTOS OF A **RIOT** THAT BROKE OUT BETWEEN TWO YOUTH **GANGS.**

I'M ON IT, BOSS!

WHEN MARTHA GETS TO THE STATION SHE HAS NO IDEA WHAT TO MAKE OF THE FRACAS AND NEITHER DO THE COPS.

TELL THE LADY WHAT YOU **HOOD-LUMS** WAS DOING...

WE WAS JUST ROCKIN'

THE JAKES CONVINCE THE KIDS TO GIVE A DEMONSTRATION OF WHAT THEY'RE TRYING TO GET-ACROSS. IMAGINE SEEING **BREAKDANCING** WITHOUT EVER KNOWING IT EXISTS!

MARTHA AND HENRY HAVE ALREADY FORMED A KIND-OF PARTNERSHIP SO SHE IMMEDIATELY GIVES HIM A CALL AND DESCRIBES WHAT SHE WITNESSED.

HEY, DO YOU GUYS KNOW **B-BOYS, BREAKERS**... I DON'T KNOW...

HOW 'BOUT THE **ROCK STEADY CREW**?

THE NEXT DAY, TWO OF THE CITY'S BEST B-BOYS, **CRAZY LEGS** AND **FROSTY FREEZE** SHOW UP AT HENRY'S STUDIO.

I MADE UP A **SPECIAL** BACKSPIN. WANNA SEE IT?

POWER MOVE

THE SUICIDE

CRAZY

IN THE LATE '70S/EARLY '80S THE IMPECCABLE **DJ JAZZY JASE** RULED **HOLLIS, QUEENS** AS A PRIME FIGURE IN THE TWO-FIFTH'S DOWN POSSE.

IN THOSE **HUMBLE**, EARLY DAYS, **DJ RUN** GAVE JASE A SOLEMN PROMISE...

WHENEVER I GET ME A **REKKID DEAL** I'M BRINGING YOU WITH ME.

UH HUH...

WHEN **RUN-DMC** SELLS A WHOPPING **250,000** COPIES OF THEIR FIRST SINGLE **IT'S LIKE THAT/ SUCKER MC'S**, THEIR LABEL **PROFILE RECORDS** IS VERY EAGER TO KEEP THE STREAK GOING.

WAR GOIN' ON ACROSS THE **SEA!**

STREET SOLDIERS KILLIN' THE **ELDERLY**...

RUSHING THE NEW SINGLE **HARD TIMES** OUT ASAP, DJ RUN MAKES GOOD ON HIS PROMISE AND ON THE **B-SIDE** RUN-DMC LETS THE WORLD KNOW THAT THERE'S A CRUCIAL THIRD MEMBER OF THE CREW. IN THE CHAOS, **DJ JAZZY JASE** MORPHS INTO...

JAM MASTER JAY!!!

THE BIG BEAT BLASTER!!

HARD TIMES/JAM MASTER JAY QUICKLY SELLS ABOUT 150,000 COPIES PROMPTING THE LABEL TO CONSIDER THE POSSIBILITY OF PRODUCING AN ENTIRE ALBUM. RUN-DMC'S MANAGER RUSSELL "RUSH" SIMMONS HAS RESERVATIONS.

EVERY RAP ALBUM OUT ITH GAW-BITCH! JUTHT CRAMMED TOGETHER BULL CRAP!

IT'TH GONNA TAKE THUM MONEY TO DO IT UP PROPPAH!

CONTRACTUALLY, WE HAVE THE RIGHT TO DO WHATEVER WE THINK IS NECESSARY, SO...

RUSSELL SIMMONS IS A RECURRING PLAYER IN THIS 1983 RAP MUSIC LANDSCAPE WITH HIS COMPANY RUSH ARTIST MANAGEMENT. HE REPRESENTS AND/OR PRODUCES MANY ARTISTS ACROSS SEVERAL LABELS.

KURTIS BLOW (MERCURY RECORDS) IS THE ARTIST RUSH CUT HIS TEETH WITH IN THE EARLY DAYS, BUT HE'S FAILED TO PRODUCE ANOTHER HIT ON THE SAME SCALE AS THE BREAKS.

IT'S PARTY ♪ TIME! ♫

WHOA, IT'S ♪ PARTYYY TIME! ♫

YOU'LL RECOGNIZE THIS BEASTIE BOYS SAMPLE

"PARTY TIME" IS NOTEWORTHY FOR IT'S FUSION OF RAP AND GO GO MUSIC

HEY LADIES!

ON PROFILE RECORDS ALONG WITH RUN-DMC IS DR. JECKYLL & MR. HYDE THEIR 1983 EFFORT GETTIN' MONEY DOESN'T HAVE THE IMPACT AS THEIR FAMOUS JAM GENIUS RAP

GETTIN' MONEY, GETTIN' MONEY! EVERY-THING IS FUNNY WHEN YOU'RE GETTIN' MONEY!

JECKYLL YEARS LATER BECOMES THE CEO OF MOTOWN

SUPER RHYMES HIMSELF, JIMMY SPICER HAS A MODEST, CASH-THEMED RECORD ALSO CALLED MONEY (DOLLAR BILL Y'ALL) ON SPRING RECORDS, THE LABEL RESPONSIBLE FOR RE-LEASING THE FIRST RAP RECORD, KING TIM III +

ADOPTED BY THE WU-TANG CLAN

...DOLLAH DOLLAH BILL, Y'ALL!

TO THE B, I, DOUBLE L, BILL, HIT IT!!

RUSS ALSO REPRESENTS A HIP HOP PIONEER, MAYBE THE GUY WHO INVENTED THE TERM HIP HOP, LOVEBUG STARSKI ON FEVER RECORDS. UNFORTUNATELY, HIS PARTY-ROCKIN' STYLE DOESN'T TRANSLATE VERY WELL ON WAX.

YOU'VE GOTTA BELIEVE!*

* YES, MARKY MARK AND THE FUNKY BUNCH SAMPLED THIS

TO ADD EVEN MORE **CASH** AND **CLOUT** TO **RUSSELL SIMMONS'** WAR-CHEST AND REPUTATION, SIMMONS SEES A TRICKLING OF THE MONEY **KURTIS BLOW** MAKES AS A **PRODUCER** FOR DIFFERENT ACTS.

FEARLESS FOUR, PROBLEMS OF THE WORLD TODAY

PROBLEMS...

NEGLECTED!

PROBLEMS...

KLEPTO !!!

SWEET G, GAMES PEOPLE PLAY

...IF THE GAME AIN'T **DRUGS**...

...IT GOT TO BE **BOOZE**...

GIGOLETTE, GAMES FEMALES PLAY

I'M GONNA PLAY THOSE GAMES ON YOU!

AT THIS STAGE IN THE GAME IT'S APPARENT THAT THERE'S AT LEAST A **NICHE MARKET** FOR RAP MUSIC, WHICH MEANS THAT NEW LABELS ARE STARTING TO SPRING UP. **VINCENT DAVIS**, FOR INSTANCE, HAS A NEW EFFORT AFFECTIONATELY TITLED **VINTERTAINMENT** THAT RELEASED TWO RECORDS BY **THE B-BOYS— TWO, THREE, BREAK** AND **ROCK THE HOUSE/CUTTIN' HERBIE.**

GORGEOUS PRETTY FLY GIRLS...

...TOURISTS FROM AROUND THE WORLD...

THE B-BOYS CONSISTS OF **DJ CHUCK CHILLOUT** AND EMCEE **DONALD D.**

CHUCK CHILLOUT IS A PROMINENT RADIO DJ ON THE SAME STATION AS **KOOL DJ RED ALERT**, **98.7 KISS FM.**

KOOL DJ RED ALERT

MR. MAGIC

CHUCK CHILLOUT

WBLS 107.5 →

MARLEY MARL

VINTERTAINMENT CONTINUES TO OCCASIONALLY DOLE OUT RECORDS OVER THE YEARS, MAYBE THE BIGGEST HIT IS 1986'S **PEE-WEE'S DANCE** BY **JOESKI LOVE.**

CHECK IT OUT PARTY PEOPLE 'CUZ THIS PARTY IS **BURNIN'**, FOR A NEW DANCE I KNOW YOU BEEN **YEARNIN'**...

THIS IS FOR ALL YOU PEOPLE **CONCERNIN'**, A BRAND NEW DANCE CALLED THE **PEE-WEE HERMAN.**

IF YOU LOOK CLOSE ENOUGH WHILE WATCHING THE PEE-WEE DANCE MUSIC VIDEO YOU WILL SPOT AN ALMOST FAMOUS **ICE-T.**

WHEN *ICE T* BECOMES A STAR HE ENLISTS THE B-BOY'S *DONALD D* FIRST AS A GUEST EMCEE, THEN AS A CO-PRODUCER IN HIS COLLECTIVE/LABEL *RHYME SYNDICATE.*

DARLENE

EVIL E

LATELY **MICHAEL HOLMAN** IS PUTTING A LOT OF THOUGHT INTO WHAT HE **MAY** HAVE DONE BY INTRODUCING **MALCOLM MCLAREN** AND **RUZA BLUE** TO **HIP HOP CULTURE.** *

...POSSIBLE **CULTURE VULTURES...**

...ARE THEY GOING TO **CLAIM** HIP HOP AS THEIR **OWN**? LIKE THEY DID WITH **PUNK ROCK**?

...SO MANY PEOPLE THINK PUNK WAS A UK INVENTION. THEY DON'T EVEN KNOW **THE RAMONES... TELEVISION...**

I'LL BE DAMNED!

HOLMAN IS A CHILD OF THE '60S AND REMEMBERS THE IMPACT OF DANCE/MUSIC PROGRAMS LIKE **SHINDIG!, AMERICAN BANDSTAND**, AND **HULLABALOO.**

I KNOW CABLE TV ISN'T AVAILABLE IN TOO MANY NEIGHBORHOODS YET, BUT I JUST GOT A SLOT TO DO MY OWN **CABLE ACCESS SHOW.**

BUTTER, YO!

PRINCE VINCE GALLO

MICHAEL CREATES SEVERAL SHOWS FOR **STATION J— ON BEAT TV, NINE THIRTY SHOW**, AND **TV NEW YORK.**

TEST 1, 2, 1, 2. LIVE AND IN **ELECTRO-MAGNETIC** COLOR...

...THE HIP-HOP MUSIC SHOW THAT IS AS **FRESH** AS THE NAME...

FROM **DOWNTOWN MANHATTAN TV NEW YORK.**

A FEW HIGHLIGHTS FROM THE VARIOUS PROGRAMS

THERE'S A GREAT PIECE SHOWCASING **DJ JAZZY JAY** 'S VIRTUOSITY FROM A NIGHTCLUB JAM.

HIGHLY ACCLAIMED IN THE **BRONX** AS ONE OF THE BEST SPECIAL MIX DJS...

DJ JAZZY JAY AT THE SIDE OF **AFRIKA BAMBAATAA** OF THE **ZULU NATION**

PENROD

BEAT BOP'S **K-ROB** * BUSTS A **MANIC** FREE-STYLE WITH **DJ HIGH PRIEST** ON THE WHEELS OF STEEL.

HIGH PRIEST WAS IN A BAND CALLED "GRAY" WITH HOLMAN, BASQUIAT AND PRINCE VINCE

* HHFT BOOK 2, --EGOMANIACAL ED

FUTURA 2000 IS CAPTURED PAINTING A MURAL ALL THE WHILE B-BOYS AND B-GIRLS GET WILD TO POPULAR BREAKS.

WATCHING FUTURA PAINT MECHANICALLY PERFECT ARCHES FREEHAND IS A SIGHT TO BEHOLD!

FAB FIVE FREDDY'S APPEARANCE IS A MEMORABLE ONE WITH POPPERS AND LOCKERS FLANKING HIM, AND THE SUCKER MC'S INSTRUMENTAL UNDERNEATH HIS VOCALS.

SO LAY YOUR CARDS ON THE TABLE AN' PLACE YOUR BET! I BETCHA ALL THIS IS SOMETHIN' YOU AIN'T HEARD YET.

'CUZ IT'S FINE, DIVINE, LIKE VINTAGE WINE...

...AND BEST OF ALL, YES Y'ALL IT'S GEN-YOU-WINE!

'CUZ IT'S ME YOU SEE FAB FIVE FRED-DEE...

...THE NAME YOU HEARD ON RAPTURE BY BLONDIE!

TO EVERY HOME VIEWER'S ASTONISHMENT, GRANDMIXER DST BEAT-JUGGLES KURTIS BLOW'S RECORD TOUGH, KNOCKING THE CROWD ON THEIR BUTTS.

WHY HAS IT GOTTA BE...

SO WHY HAS IT GOT TO BE...

THE GRANDMAN ON THE BANDSTAND
GRANDMIXER D.ST.

THIS CABLE ACCESS THING IS GOOD PRACTICE, BUT I NEED TO SEE ABOUT GETTING A HIP HOP TV SHOW OUT THERE ON A NATIONAL LEVEL.

DEF, WORD, YO!

IN THE LATE '70S/EARLY '80S **AARON FUCHS** MAKES HIS BONES AS A FREELANCE MUSIC CRITIC.

YOU OWE ME FIVE DOLLARS...

...I TOLD YOU THAT **AL GREEN** WAS GONNA BLOW UP...

WITH A KEEN EYE ON THE MUSIC BIZ AND GOOD HISTORICAL UNDERSTANDING OF OUR CULTURE, FUCHS POSTULATES...

PAUL WINLEY RECORDS

...ISN'T IT INTERESTING THAT THESE OLD, HARLEM **DOO-WOP** RECORD LABELS ARE NOW DOING **RAP RECORDS**?

ENJOY RECORDS

AFRIKA BAMBAATAA

GRANDMASTER FLASH

AARON CONVINCES HIMSELF THAT HE'S NOT SO OLD THAT HE CAN'T TAKE SOME RISKS. HE FORMS **TUFF CITY RECORDS** AND RECRUITS FELLOW **VILLAGE VOICE** WRITER **BARRY MICHAEL COOPER** TO CONSTRUCT A TANDEM OF RECORDS THAT SKEW MORE TOWARD THE **ELECTRO** SIDE OF THE SPECTRUM.

IN FACT, ON THE HEELS OF THE SUCCESS WITH **PLANET ROCK**, **AFRIKA BAMBAATAA** AGREED TO MIX THE SMURPH RECORD AT A DISCOUNT.

THE **COLD CRUSH BROTHERS** NEVER GOT THEY DUE YET. I'LL BRING 'EM BY. LETCHOO MEET 'EM...

WHEN **BARRY MICHAEL COOPER** DISCOVERS AARON FUCHS WANTS TO MAKE A MORE TRADITIONAL RAP RECORD...

HOW LONG YOU KNOW ME?

YOU DIDN'T KNOW THAT **SPOONIE GEE** IS MY ACE?

ON THE STRENGTH OF THE ABOVE TWO RECORDS FUCHS IS ABLE TO NEGOTIATE A DISTRIBUTION DEAL WITH CONGLOMERATE **CBS** RECORDS.

THE FIRST RECORD THAT IS PART OF THIS NEW DEAL IS **PUNK ROCK RAP** BY THE **COLD CRUSH BROTHERS**. AS THE TITLE IMPLIES IT'S SORT OF A NOVELTY RECORD BUILT TO CAPITALIZE ON THE **DOWNTOWN** CONVERGENCE OF THESE TWO WORLDS THANKS TO PEOPLE LIKE **FAB FIVE FREDDY** AND **MALCOLM MCLAREN**.

QUEUE UP PUNK ROCK RAP AND YOU MAY RECOGNIZE THE OFT-SAMPLED WOMAN AT THE VERY BEGINNING.

OH MY GOD!

IT'S THE COLD CRUSH!!

MOST NOTABLY THE "OH MY GOD" RIFF WAS MADE FAMOUS BY **DOUG E. FRESH AND THE GET FRESH CREW'S** 1985 SMASH HIT, **THE SHOW**.

SIX MINUTES...

QUICK CLICK CLICK

SIX MINUTES...

QUICK CLICK CLICK

SIX MINUTES, DOUG E. FRESH, YER ON!

THE SECOND **TUFF CITY/CBS** RECORD IS **SPOONIE GEE'S THE BIG BEAT** WHICH GETS THE RAPPER SOME SHINE AFTER A YEAR-LONG STASIS AT THE HAND OF HIS PREVIOUS LABEL, **SUGAR HILL**.

WHETHER YOU'RE **MEAN** OR IF YOU'RE **SWEET**, THIS YOU CAN'T RESIST...

...IT'S THE BIG BEAT!

NEITHER "PUNK ROCK RAP" OR "THE BIG BEAT" GET MUCH ATTENTION OR PROMOTION BY THE PARENT COMPANY, **CBS**. THE CORPORATION IS TOO BUSY DEALING WITH A **PHENOMENON** ON THEIR HANDS.

EPILOGUE/FUN FACT/TRIVIAL MINUTIAE: THAT EARLY **TUFF CITY** PRODUCER **BARRY MICHAEL COOPER** WROTE A FEW ARTICLES, INCLUDING ONE ON **TEDDY RILEY**, THAT CAUGHT THE ATTENTION OF **HOLLY-WOOD**, EARNING HIM THE OPPORTUNITY TO CRAFT SCREEN-PLAYS BEGINNING WITH **NEW JACK CITY**.

I WANNA SHOOT YOU SO BAD, MY **DICK'S HARD!**

ICE T

NINO BROWN

SO FAR WE'VE SEEN A FEW FUTURE ITERATIONS OF **ICE T'S** CAREER, BUT IF YOU'RE CURIOUS ABOUT WHAT HE'S UP TO IN THIS YEAR OF **1983** YOU DON'T HAVE TO LOOK BEYOND A SMALL DOCUMENTARY CALLED **BREAKIN' AND ENTERIN'.**

HIP HOPPIN' IS THE THING THAT'S **IN,** IT'S WHERE THE STONE COLD, NITRO PARTY **BEGINS...**

...SO LISTEN PARTY PEOPLE WITH YOUR EARS TO THE **STREETS,** THE COLLEGE PROFESSORS AND THE SOCIAL **ELITE...**

...TO THE FLY YOUNG GUYS AND THE PRETTY **GIRLS,** ICE T IS GONNA TELL YOU 'BOUT THE HIP HOP **WORLD...**

THE EPICENTER OF THE FILM IS THE **RADIOTRON COMMUNITY CENTER** IN THE **MACARTHUR PARK** AREA OF **LOS ANGELES.**

EGYPTIAN LOVER

CHRIS "THE GLOVE" TAYLOR

ONLY LA MEMBER OF ZULU NATION

ICE T

WEST COAST HIP HOP TAKES A MUCH DIFFERENT FORM THAN IN NEW YORK. IT'S MUCH MORE DANCE-CENTRIC AND IS LARGELY THE FOCUS OF BREAKIN' AND ENTERIN'.

THE BLUE CITY CREW

WILL SOON BECOME THE BOO-YAA TRIBE!!

TOPPER CAREW, THE PRODUCER OF THE FILM, MAKES SURE TO HIGHLIGHT DEMONSTRATIONS BY TWO OF THE MOST SUCCESSFUL DANCERS IN THE SCENE.

HI, I'M **SHABBA DOO.** I'M ONE OF THE ORIGINAL **LOCKERS.** I STARTED IN 1972...

BOOGALOO SHRIMP

TO START OFF YOUR BREAKING YOU DO A PREP...

...IT'S CALLED THE **UPROCK.**

BY DAY AT THE **RADIOTRON COMMUNITY CENTER**, ICE T AND THE **RADIO CREW** TEACH THE YOUTH HOW TO RAP, POP AND LOCK.

THERE ARE ACTUALLY QUITE A FEW SEGMENTS WITH **T** IN RAP CYPHERS WITH ELEMENTARY SCHOOL KIDS.

TEESHA, YA DON'T QUIT, KICK UP THE BEAT TO THE **ULTIMATE**...

MY NAME IS **TEESHA**, I'M AN ITTY-BITTY **BABE**, WHEN IT COMES TO LOVE I'M A FULL GROWN **LADY**...

ALL THESE KIDS HAVE ART IN 'EM... RUNNIN' THROUGH THEIR BODIES. THEY WANNA BE ARTISTS. THEY'RE EITHER DANCERS OR GRAFFITI PAINTERS OR THEY BUILD MODELS OR SOMETHIN'...

...BUT MOST OF THE COMMUNITY AND THE PEOPLE OUT THERE WON'T GIVE THEM ANY RESPECT FOR THAT...

...THEY JUST WANT TO SAY THAT THEY'RE **JUVENILE DELINQUENTS**.

BREAKIN' AND ENTERIN' NEVER RECEIVED MUCH, IF ANY, PLAY IN THE STATES BUT WAS RELEASED TO A CULT FOLLOWING IN **GERMANY** UNDER THE TITLE **BREAKDANCE GANG**.

IN **1985** THE RADIOTRON BUILDING IS CONDEMNED FOR NOT MEETING STRICT, NEW, **EARTHQUAKE** CODES.

CHARLIE STETTLER IS A FORMER SWISS SOCCER STAR AND BORN HUSTLER. HE'S THE KIND OF GUY WHO CAN SELL WATER TO A WHALE. HIS SCHEME DUJOUR IS TIN PAN APPLE, AN AUDIO CASSETTE HE CREATED FULL OF ENVIRONMENTAL NEW YORK CITY NOISES AND HE'S GOING TO GREAT LENGTHS TO MAKE IT A SUCCESS.

THE HARD WORK PAYS OFF AS MANY MAJOR STORES AND TOURIST TRAPS PUT IN ORDERS FOR THE TAPE.

WE SOLD OVER 250,000 COPIES SO FAR!

THE NEXT LOGICAL MOVE IS TO DO A RAP SEQUEL TO TRY AND CAPITALIZE. TIN PAN APPLE/AFTER DARK TURNS OUT TO BE A DUD.

I HAVE AN IDEA...

...WE'LL BE ABLE TO SELL WAY MORE RECORDS IF WE CAN FIGURE OUT SOME SORT OF RAP CONTEST PROMOTION WITH SOME STIPULATION THAT THE PERFORMERS MUST RHYME OVER THE INSTRUMENTAL TO OUR RECORD!

STETTLER AND HIS PARTNER, LYNDA WEST RUN TO MR. MAGIC'S RADIO STATION 107.5 WBLS TO TRY AND RAISE AWARENESS TO THEIR PLAN.

RADIO IS A BUSINESS OF ADVERTISING.

YOU GET A CORPORATE SPONSOR AND WE'LL PROMOTE YOU ALL DAY.

FOLLOWING A FEW LEADS CHARLIE STETTLER HEADS TO THE OFFICES OF COCA-COLA.

WE WON'T BE A PART OF ANY EVENT THAT TAKES PLACE IN A VENUE SMALLER THAN RADIO CITY MUSIC HALL.

WE WERE THINKING OF HAVING THE FINALS AT STUDIO 54, BUT RADIO CITY WON'T BE A PROBLEM.

TIN PAN APPLE RAP AND DANCE CONTEST

19

CHARLIE **IMMEDIATELY** ISSUES A PRESS RELEASE THANKING **COCA COLA** FOR THEIR **$300,000** CONTRIBUTION JUST IN CASE THE SODA MANUFACTURER GETS SECOND THOUGHTS.

THITH ITH BIG ENOUGH THAT I WANT THUMMA MY AWTITHT INVOLVED.

WORD QUICKLY TRAVELS ACROSS THE FIVE BOROUGHS AND PRELIMINARY CONTESTS BEGIN SPRINGING UP ALL OVER THE CITY AT GYMS, CLUBS, AND SKATING RINKS. **TIN PAN APPLE/AFTER DARK** SELLS THE **THOUSANDS** OF RECORDS CHARLIE HOPED FOR.

LOTS OF **PROFESSIONAL** TALENT GETS INTO THE SPIRIT AS EITHER SHOW HOSTS OR JUDGES.

MR. MAGIC

WHODINI

KURTIS BLOW

FEARLESS FOUR

WITHIN A FEW WEEKS ALL OF THE **FINALISTS** ACROSS TOWN ARE CHOSEN FOR THE SHOW AT **RADIO CITY MUSIC HALL** THAT IS SCHEDULED TO TAKE PLACE **MAY 23 1983** DAYS BEFORE THE EVENT IS TO HAPPEN **CHARLIE STETTLER** AND HIS CREW ARE SUMMONED TO THE **VENUE** BY SEVERAL **UNION HEADS.**

WE DON'T WANT **NIGGERS** IN OUR BUILDING.

ALL MY GUYS ARE GONNA COME DOWN WITH THE **FLU** THE DAY OF YOUR SHOW.

JUST SO YOU KNOW I AM PREPARING A PRESS CONFERENCE TO REPEAT EVERYTHING WE DISCUSS TODAY. ARE WE DONE HERE?

I'LL SEE YOU ALL ON THE WEEKEND.

20

THE **CONTEST** STILL TAKES PLACE ON ITS SCHEDULED DAY THOUGH THERE ARE A FEW **CONTINGENCIES** THAT NEED TO BE ADDRESSED.

THE MAIN **CHALLENGE** IS THAT NO REGULAR STAFF FROM **RADIO CITY MUSIC HALL** COMES TO WORK THE EVENT. THANKFULLY, **SAL ABBATIELLO** BRINGS HIS SECURITY FORCE FROM THE **DISCO FEVER** NIGHTCLUB TO KEEP THE **6,000** YOUTHS IN ATTENDANCE SAFE AND SOUND.

THERE'S ALSO A SMATTERING OF **IMPRESARIOS** AMONGST THE CROWD.

THITH AIN'T BAD, RIGHT, THOOKI?

'SOKAY.

MASTERFUL **MR. MAGIC** IS THE HOST EMCEE FOR THE **TIN PAN APPLE RAP AND DANCE CONTEST.**

LISTEN UP...

CHILL WITH THE FOOLISH- NESS...

THE **PROMISE** TO THE WINNER OF THE RAP CONTEST IS A **RECORD CONTRACT** SO IT MAKES SENSE THAT THE JUDGES WOULD BE THE **OWNERS** OF POPULAR RAP LABELS.

SYLVIA ROBINSON SUGAR HILL RECORDS

TOM SILVERMAN TOMMY BOY

TRUTHFULLY, THERE IS **NO** RECORD DEAL IN PLACE, BUT THE EVENT ORGANIZER **CHARLIE STETTLER** ISN'T SWEATING IT. RIGHT NOW HE'S HAPPY WITH TODAY'S **SUCCESS.**

IT WOULD BE HARDER **NOT** TO GET A **RECORD DEAL** FOR THESE KIDS...

21

THE WINNERS OF THE **BREAKDANCE** PORTION OF THE SHOW ARE A TRIO OF B-BOYS CALLED **UTFO** (**UNTOUCHABLE FORCE ORGANIZATION**). HISTORY MAKES IT UNCLEAR WHAT THEY WIN EXACTLY. THEIR PROFILE CLEARLY SKYROCKETS GETTING THEM EXPOSURE FIRST VIA **THE PHIL DONAHUE SHOW** AND THEN THEY QUICKLY BECOME BACK-UP DANCERS ON TOUR FOR **WHODINI**.

THE **RAP CONTEST WINNERS** AND ABSOLUTE **UNANIMOUS** CROWD **FAVORITES** ARE A **TRIO** OF **ROTUND MALE ADOLESCENTS** WHO CALL THEMSELVES THE **DISCO THREE**.

22

THE **DISCO THREE** CONSISTS OF...

| KOOL ROCK-SKI | PRINCE MARKIE DEE | BIG BUFF LOVE/ DJ DOC NICE/ THE HUMAN BEATBOX |

NO **MAJOR** RECORD LABELS ARE KNOCKING DOWN DOORS TO GET TO THE **DISCO THREE**, BUT AS **CHARLIE STETTLER** ANTICIPATED IT ISN'T TOO HARD TO FIND A HOME FOR HIS BOYS. **SUTRA RECORDS** RELEASES THEIR **DEBUT** SINGLE "**REALITY**." YOU WOULD BE CORRECT IN ASSUMING BY THE TITLE THAT THEIR SONG SKEWS TOWARD THE TREND ESTABLISHED BY **THE MESSAGE** BY **GRANDMASTER FLASH AND THE FURIOUS FIVE** OF RHYMING ABOUT EVERYDAY STRUGGLES.

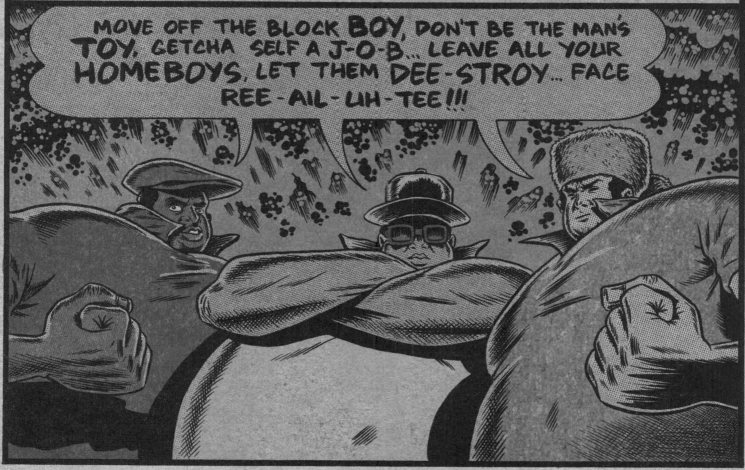

MOVE OFF THE BLOCK **BOY**, DON'T BE THE MAN'S **TOY**, GETCHA SELF A J-O-B... LEAVE ALL YOUR **HOMEBOYS**, LET THEM DEE-STROY... FACE REE-AIL-UH-TEE!!!

THE **DIDACTIC**, HEAVY-HANDED DISCO THREE RECORD IS A LEAD-BALLOON, BUT **STETTLER** DOESN'T DESPAIR. HE WANTS TO TRY A BIT OF TEST MARKETING WITH THE TRIO IN HIS HOMELAND OF **SWITZERLAND**.

IF YOU GUYS CAN GET A RESPONSE FROM THESE **YODELING ASSHOLES** THEN I KNOW WE HAVE SOMETHING **SPECIAL**.

THESE **PEANUTS** IS **FREE**?

IN **ZURICH**, STETTLER BOOKS THE **DISCO THREE** ON A FEW LOCAL NEWS PROGRAMS TO EXAMINE THE REACTION OF THE AUDIENCE.

NAW, WE **NEVER** BEEN IN A AIRPLANE BEFORE.

I ONLY EVER BEEN TO **MANHATTAN** THAT **ONCE**.

THE **BOYS** HAVE CERTAINLY **NEVER** STAYED AT A HOTEL EITHER. **EACH TIME** STETTLER DISAPPEARS ON BUSINESS...

...SO IF YOU CALL DOWNSTAIRS THEY JUST WILL BRING FOOD TO US!

BET!

WE **ROCK-STARS** NOW, MAN!

CHARLIE SPENDS THAT TIME GETTING THE DISCO THREE A SHOT AT PERFORMING AT THE TOWN'S BIG **YODELING FESTIVAL** HIGH IN THE MOUNTAINS WITH A CROWD FULL OF **FARMERS**.

POP POP POP POP POP POP POP

THE RAPPERS ARE A HIT TO STETTLER'S DELIGHT, BUT THOSE GOOD FEELINGS **DIMINISH** ONCE IT'S TIME TO CHECK OUT OF THE **HOTEL**.

A 380 FR ROOM SERVICE BILL?!!

YOU MOTHERFUCKING **FAT BOYS** !!!

WHO'S FAT?

YER MOMMA'S FAT!

24

ANYONE WITHIN EARSHOT OF **MICHAEL HOLMAN** HEARS THE WHOLE SPIEL ABOUT GETTING MORE **HIP HOP** ON **TELEVISION**.

...I'M SAYIN', IF **DON CORNELIUS** DOESN'T RESPECT US THEN WE DON'T NEED **SOUL TRAIN.**

WE'LL MAKE OUR **OWN** THING!!

HOLMAN FANCIES HIMSELF A BIT OF AN **IMPRESARIO** AND HE PROMOTES DIFFERENT KINDS OF HIP HOP EVENTS AT VENUES LIKE **NEGRIL.** HIS IDEAS CATCH THE ATTENTION OF A FEW **INVESTMENT BANKERS** WHO STRUCK GOLD HELPING OUT THE GROUP **NEW EDITION.**

TO SELL THE IDEA TO THE NETWORK **STIFFS** YOU SHOULD HAVE SOME **TEST FOOTAGE.**

...NEARLY **IMPOSSIBLE** TO SELL A **PILOT** SIGHT UNSEEN.

HOLMAN WORKS WITH **AFRIKA BAMBAATAA** TO SECURE THE **BRONX RIVER COMMUNITY CENTER** FOR A HUGE DANCE PARTY TO PRODUCE A SAMPLE REEL FOR NETWORK HONCHO'S TO CHECK OUT.

RELAX, Y'ALL! YOU'LL GET YOUR **FLAMERS** AN' SHIT BACK AFTER THE SHOW!!

COME IN **PEACE,** BROTHERS.

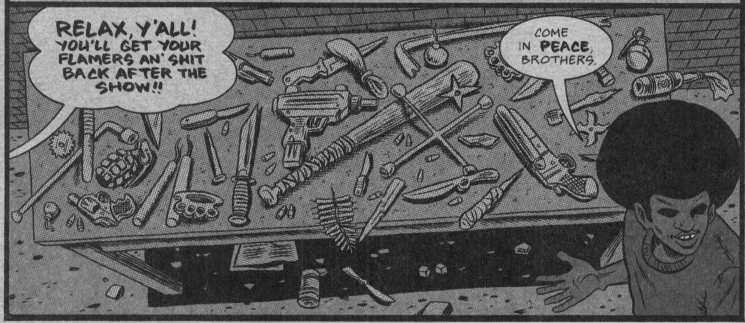

THE **A-LIST** LINEUP OF TALENT LIKE **BAM, DJ JAZZY JAY, KOOL DJ RED ALERT, THE COLD CRUSH BROTHERS,** AND THE **FORCE MCS** IS PRACTICALLY INCIDENTAL. THE JOINT GETS PACKED TIGHT ONCE WORD SPREADS THAT CAMERAS WILL BE SHOOTING ALL NIGHT.

THE CROWD IS THE MAIN FOCUS, TOO, SINCE THE VISION IS TO CREATE AN **AMERICAN BAND-STAND**-TYPE PROGRAM FOR **HIP HOP**.

HOURS AND **HOURS** AND **HOURS** OF FOOTAGE GETS TRIMMED INTO A CONCISE 7-MINUTE CUT THAT HOLMAN AFFECTIONATELY TITLES...

Graffiti Rock!
©1983

MICHAEL PUTS THE TAPE INTO THE HANDS OF EVERY TV AND AD EXEC WHO WILL LET HIM PAST SECURITY...

THOSE DANCERS ARE CERTAINLY... INTERESTING.

WE'LL... AH... BE IN TOUCH, MICHAEL. HOWZAT SOUND? M'KAY, TAKE CARE NOW.

..but...

THE **FOOTAGE** ISN'T A TOTAL WASTE. IT'S A GREAT DOCUMENT OF THE ERA AND **HOLMAN** BEGINS TO LICENSE THE MATERIAL. THE BULK OF THE **PLANET ROCK** MUSIC VIDEO IS COMPOSED OF **GRAFFITI ROCK** CLIPS, FOR INSTANCE.

YEEEEAH...

JUS' HIT ME...

MICHAEL HOLMAN DISCOVERS THAT **RICH PEOPLE** WILL OFTEN **FUND** FILMS AND ART PROJECTS AS A **TAX WRITE-OFF** SO WITH HIS SAMPLE REEL AND SOME LEGWORK HE'S ABLE TO BUILD A **$100,000** KITTY.

IT'S TOO STRONG AN IDEA TO LET GO, SO WE'LL JUST PRO-DUCE AN EPISODE AND TRY TO **SELL** IT.

DEF, WORD, FRESH, YO!

"PRINCE" VINCE GALLO

1983 IS AS PROLIFIC A YEAR AS ANY FOR **KOOL MOE DEE** AND HIS GROUP **THE TREACHEROUS THREE**. THE RELEASE **3** SINGLES THROUGH **SUGAR HILL** RECORDS: **ACTION, GET UP,** AND **TURNING YOU ON.**

IT'S AN INNOVATING, RHYME RELATING SOUND COMIN' DOWN TO THE RAP CREATING... OUT SPOKEN, ENGLISH BROKEN... BEATS THROWN TOGETHER IN A SONG THAT'S SMOKIN'!!!

CARRERA PORSCHE 5620'S

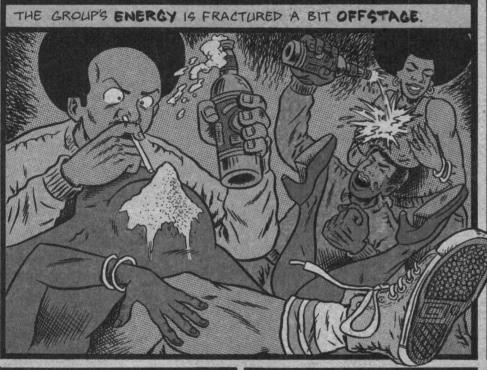

THE GROUP'S **ENERGY** IS FRACTURED A BIT **OFFSTAGE.**

WHILE **SPECIAL K** AND **L.A. SUNSHINE** WILD OUT, **KOOL MOE DEE** USES HIS EARNINGS TO PUT HIMSELF THROUGH SCHOOL AT THE **STATE UNIVERSITY OF NEW YORK.**

SUNSHINE, CAN YOU SCOOP ME UP SOME **MONEY** FROM **SUGAR HILL**? I GOT A FEW EXPENSIVE-ASS **TEXT BOOKS** THIS **SEMESTER.**

I NEED TO PICK UP SOME ENDS FOR **MYSELF** ANYWAY. I'MMA KEEP $20 FOR MY TROUBLES, **MOE.** HA HA!

YEAH? I'LL GIVE YOU 20 KICKS IN YOUR **BEHIND.** HA HA.

A FEW TRAIN RIDES AND BUS HOPS LATER...

I MUS' BE WEARIN' **MISS SYLVIA** DOWN. SHE DIDN'T GIVE ME NO **STATIC** FOR OUR **BREAD.**

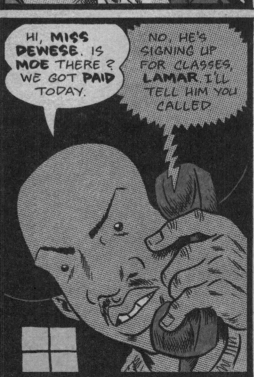

HI, **MISS DEWESE.** IS **MOE** THERE? WE GOT **PAID** TODAY.

NO, HE'S SIGNING UP FOR CLASSES, LAMAR. I'LL TELL HIM YOU CALLED

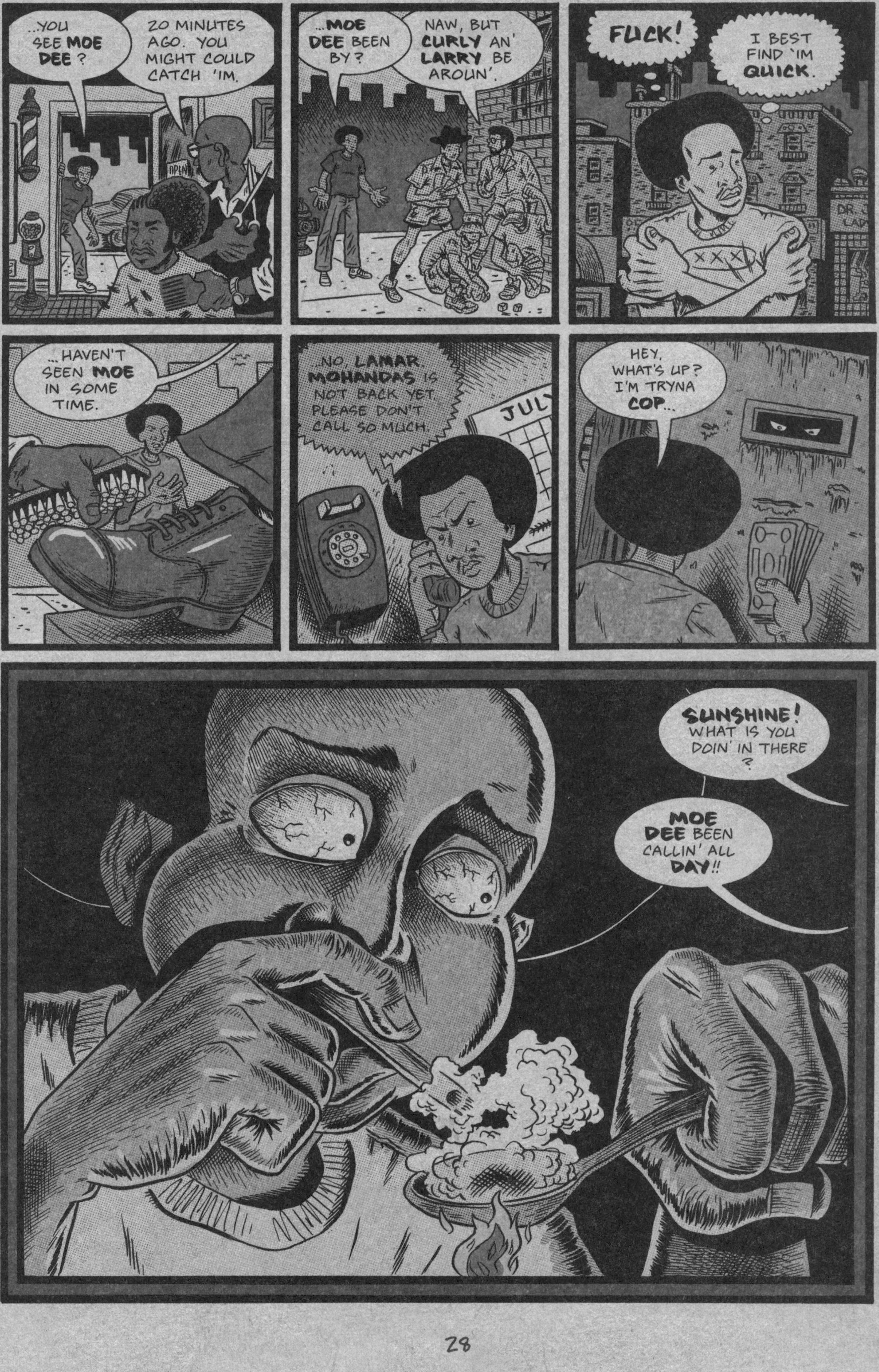
...YOU SEE MOE DEE?
20 MINUTES AGO. YOU MIGHT COULD CATCH 'IM.
OPEN
...MOE DEE BEEN BY?
NAW, BUT CURLY AN' LARRY BE AROUN'.
FUCK!
I BEST FIND 'IM QUICK.
...HAVEN'T SEEN MOE IN SOME TIME.
...NO LAMAR. MOHANDAS IS NOT BACK YET. PLEASE DON'T CALL SO MUCH.
JULY
HEY, WHAT'S UP? I'M TRYNA COP...
SUNSHINE! WHAT IS YOU DOIN' IN THERE?
MOE DEE BEEN CALLIN' ALL DAY!!

THE COMMON WISDOM OF **1983** IS THAT FULL-LENGTH RAP ALBUMS **DON'T SELL**. THEY'RE MOSTLY JUST COBBLED TOGETHER COLLECTIONS OF 12-INCH RECORDS, AND THE FEW ALBUMS THAT WERE PRODUCED WITH ORIGINAL CONTENT NEVER REALLY RECOUP THE INVESTMENT ENOUGH TO JUSTIFY MAKING MORE.

"WELCOME TO THE PLACE WHERE ALL THE CREATURES **MEET**. THE LAST BUILDING TO YOUR LEFT ON A DEAD-END **STREET**."

THE **BRITISH LABEL, JIVE RECORDS,** IS FAR ENOUGH REMOVED FROM THIS NOTION THAT THEY FLY **WHODINI** TO ENGLAND TO CREATE THEIR **SELF-TITLED ALBUM**, WITH **THE HAUNTED HOUSE OF ROCK** AS THE HIGHLIGHT.

"YOU'LL FIND SKELETON BONES OUTSIDE ON THE **PAVEMENT**. AND TORTURE CHAMBERS DOWN IN THE **BASEMENT**."

USING STATE-OF-THE-ART EQUIPMENT LIKE THE EXPENSIVE AND RARE **FAIRLIGHT CMI, THOMAS DOLBY** AND OTHER **UK** PRODUCERS COMPOSE THE MUSIC WHILE **WHODINI** CARVES OUT THEIR OWN LYRICS.

"COBWEBS HANGIN' OVER YOUR **HEAD** AN' MUSIC BEIN' PLAYED BY THE **GRATEFUL DEAD**."

"AN' SPINNIN' ON THE TURNTABLES **BACK TO BACK** IS NO OTHER THAN MY MAIN MAN **WOLF-MAN JACK**."

THE RESULTING SOUND IS **VASTLY** DIFFERENT THAN ANYTHING BEING DONE WITH RAP MUSIC IN THE **U.S.** BUT THIS ELECTRIC, EUROPEAN VIBE ENDEARS WHODINI TO A HUGE AUDIENCE AS THEY CONTINUE TOURING ACROSS THE POND.

"THE MC OF THE NIGHT RAPPIN' TO THE **TUNES** WAS THE CREATURE FROM THE BLACK **LAGOON**."

"THERE'S A SIGN ON THE DOOR THAT CAN'T BE **MISSED**. IT READS 'ENTER... BUT AT YOUR OWN **RISK**.'"

BACK HOME IN THE STATES, **WHODINI** REFLECTS WITH **FRUSTRATION** THAT THEY COULDN'T COMMUNICATE THEIR MUSICAL IDEAS WITH THE **BRITISH-BASED** LABEL.

WHAT CAN WE DO ABOUT THIS, **MAGIC**?

SOUNDS LIKE Y'ALL CAN USE A GOOD **MANAGER** AT THIS STAGE IN THE GAME.

I KNOW A GUY.

MARLEY MARL

THE MOST ACTIVE, PROMINENT, AND INFLUENTIAL MANAGER IN RAP MUSIC IS, OF COURSE, NONE OTHER THAN **RUSSELL "RUSH" SIMMONS**.

YOU BOYTH THINE WITH ME AN' I'LL MAKE SURE YUH AWTITH'TIC VISION AIN'T COMPROMITH'D

Y'ALL FIRTH'T REKKIDTH WUTH OKAY, BUT WE NEED TO GETCH Y'ALL A THERIOTH HIP HOP PRODOOTHA!

ONCE **WHODINI** SIGNS WITH **RUSH** THEY'RE QUICKLY INTRODUCED TO THE MAN RESPONSIBLE WITH THE SOUND BEHIND THE INCREASINGLY POPULAR **RUN-DMC**. HIS NAME IS **LARRY SMITH**.

I GOT SOME STUFF IN MIND FOR Y'ALL ALREADY, 'CUZ TO BE HONEST YOUR REKKIDS DON'T IMPRESS ME...

...BUT I CAN TELL Y'ALL GOT A NUGGET OF POTENTIAL.

DISCO FEVER

REP FROM LARGE ARTS FOUNDATION

...A FILM ABOUT GRAFFITI?

WE CAN'T ENDORSE THIS.

GOVERNMENT ART FUNDERS

YOU WANT TO GLORIFY CRIMINALS?

DON'T THINK SO!

FUNDERS FOR PUBLIC TELEVISION

THIS SOUNDS FASCINATING BUT WE CAN'T BE RESPONSIBLE FOR DESTRUCTIVE BEHAVIOR.

HENRY CHALFANT, THE GRAFFITI PHOTOGRAPHER, AND FILMMAKER TONY SILVER GET INITIAL FUNDING FOR THEIR GRAFF-INSPIRED DOCUMENTARY, STYLE WARS, FROM CHANNEL 4 IN THE UK. THIS BRITISH NETWORK ALSO FUNDED THE FILM WILD STYLE THE PREVIOUS YEAR.

GIVE US LICENSE TO BROADCAST THE FILM IN OUR COUNTRY...

...AND WE CAN DO BUSINESS.

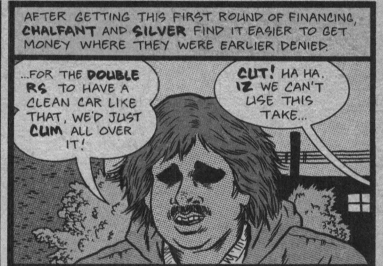

AFTER GETTING THIS FIRST ROUND OF FINANCING, CHALFANT AND SILVER FIND IT EASIER TO GET MONEY WHERE THEY WERE EARLIER DENIED.

...FOR THE DOUBLE RS TO HAVE A CLEAN CAR LIKE THAT, WE'D JUST CUM ALL OVER IT!

CUT! HA HA. IZ WE CAN'T USE THIS TAKE...

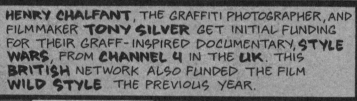

STYLE WARS IS THE PERFECT TITLE FOR THE FILM AS IT CAPTURES THE MANY STRUGGLES AND BATTLES WITHIN HIP HOP / GRAFFITI CULTURE.

DETECTIVE BERNIE JACOBS

I'M NOT AN ART CRITIC...

...BUT, I CAN SURE AS HELL TELL YOU IT'S A CRIME!

RICHARD RAVITCH, CHAIRMAN METRO TRANSPORTATION AUTHORITY

GIVE THEM ALL BROOMS...

GIVE THEM ALL SPONGES!

NYC MAYOR ED KOCH

"DUMP KOCH." THIS MEANS WE'RE GETTING TO THEM!

THE FIRST SHOOT OF THE FILM WAS THIS B-BOY BATTLE AT UNITED SKATES OF AMERICA.

DYNAMIC ROCKERS

VS.

ROCKSTEADY CREW

MANY **WRITERS** IN THE FILM STRIVE TO OUT-DO AND/OR IMPRESS EACH OTHER...

I'M THE KING OF WHAT? THE KING OF **STYYYYYLE!**

SHOOT, I GOT STYLES THAT'S ALREADY MORE COMPLEX THAT NOBODY KNOW ABOUT. **SUPER DUTY TOUGH WORK.**

THE ERSATZ **VILLAIN** OF THE DOCUMENTARY IS THE **ROGUE-BOMBER, CAP,** WHOSE PERSONAL PHILOSOPHY VALUES QUANTITY OVER QUALITY.

TO ME THE OBJECT IS **MORE!**

...NOT THE BIGGEST AND THE BEAUTIFULLEST...

...BUT, **MORE!**

THE MOST **DRAMATIC** PARTS OF THE NARRATIVE HIGHLIGHT THE REST OF THE GRAFFITI COMMUNITY'S FEELING ABOUT **CAP,** WHO SPECIALIZES IN CROSSING OUT HIS ENEMIES.

...HE WENT OVER IT LIKE **BLAH!** THAT **HURT** ME.

HE A JEALOUS **TOY** 'CAUSE HE CAN'T DO A **BURNER** AND SHIT. CAN'T EVEN DO A **STRAIGHT LETTER.**

HE DID A **CAP** THROW-UP OVER ME AND AN **MPC** OVER THIS AN' WROTE **WAR** NEXT TO **FAT ALBERT.**

YOU CAN NEVER MAKE UP FOR THAT. THAT'S **NEVER FORGIVE ACTION.**

THE BATTLE BETWEEN LEGITIMATE GRAFFITI ARTISTS AND THE DOWNTOWN FINE ARTS COMMUNITY GETS SOME ILLUMINATION IN **STYLE WARS.**

IT'S ALMOST AS THOUGH THESE PIECES WERE PEELED OFF THE TRAIN AND PUT ONTO **CANVAS.**

PARENTAL DISAPPROVAL IS AN OBVIOUS COMPONENT OF THE GRAFFITI WORLD AND THE **EXCHANGES** BETWEEN **SKEME** AND HIS **MOTHER** ARE **UNFORGETTABLE.**

I DIDN'T WRITE TO GO TO **PARIS.** I STARTED WRITING TO **BOMB.** TO DESTROY ALL LINES.

SEE WHAT I'M SAYING WHEN I SAY I DON'T **UNDERSTAND** HIM? WHAT HAVE THE LINES **EVER** DONE TO **HIM?**

JUST A PORTION OF THE **STYLE WARS** SOUNDTRACK...

FEARLESS 4: ROCKIN' IT

SUGARHILL GANG: 8TH WONDER

GRANDMASTER FLASH AND THE FURIOUS FIVE: THE MESSAGE

TREACHEROUS THREE: FEEL THE HEARTBEAT

TROUBLE FUNK: PUMP ME UP

RAMMELLZEE VS. K-ROB: BEAT BOP

DION: THE WANDERER

MANY OF THE KIDS INTERVIEWED IN **STYLE WARS** GO ONTO SOME PRETTY GREAT THINGS IN THE HIP HOP WORLD. TAKE **REVOLT** HERE, FOR INSTANCE...

HE'S DONE A TON OF ART FOR DIFFERENT MUSICIANS OF ALL SORTS.

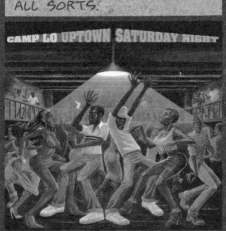

THIS DESIGN MAY BE HIS MOST **FAMOUS** CREATION.

ZEPHYR

...THEY'RE BEATING THE SYSTEM...

ZEPHYR CREATED THE OPENING ANIMATION AND CO-STARRED IN **WILD STYLE** HE'S CONTINUED PROMOTING GRAFFITI AS A FOREFATHER OF THE MEDIUM THROUGH EXHIBITS, LECTURES, ARTICLES, AND BOOKS.

MARE 139

CAP? I DON'T KNOW...

...SOME BIG **WHITE BOY**...

MARE IS ONE OF THE MANY WHO MOVED TO SCULPTURE AS A CREATIVE OUTLET. HE DESIGNED THE **BET/BLACK ENTERTAINMENT AWARD.**

DEZ

EXTRA-TELLEST, WE THE BEST!!

WHEN SUBWAY GRAFFITI DRIED UP **DEZ** GOT INTO A LIFESTYLE THAT LEAD TO PRISON. WHEN HE GOT OUT HE BECAME A PROMINENT MIX TAPE DJ.

HE'S EASY TO MISS IF YOU'RE NOT PAYING ATTENTION, BUT **CEY ADAMS** IS IN THE FILM CLEAR AS DAY DURING THE ART GALLERY SEQUENCE.

I'M INTO MAKIN' MONEY!

CEY'S CREDITS RUN DEEP. HE MIGHT BE THE PREEMINENT ARTIST/GRAPHIC DESIGNER IN HIP HOP. AT THIS EARLY STAGE IN THE GAME, THOUGH, THIS MAY BE HIS MOST VISIBLE LOGO.

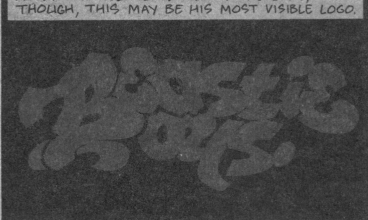

34

THE **STYLE WARS** DOCUMENTARY BROADCASTS NATIONALLY ON **PBS** IN **1983** BUT THERE IS ALSO A VERY MEMORABLE THEATER SCREENING IN **NYC**.

WILD STYLE
STYLE WARS

WILD STYLE HAD BEEN RUNNING HERE FOR SOME TIME AND WITH **STYLE WARS** ROUNDING OUT THIS SOLID **DOUBLE-FEATURE**, BUSINESS IS **GREAT**.

WELCOME ONE AND ALL!

ENJOY! ENJOY!!

REMEMBER, KIDS, THE LARGE POPCORN IS THE BEST VALUE FOR YA BUCK!

STYLE WARS DIRECTOR, **TONY SILVER**, HAS TO INDEPENDENTLY RENT AND RUN THE NECESSARY **16MM** PROJECTOR FOR THIS OCCASION.

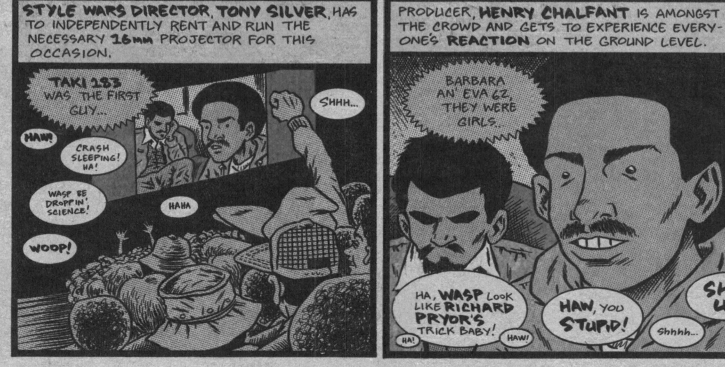

TAKI 183 WAS THE FIRST GUY...

SHHH...

HAW!

CRASH SLEEPING! HA!

WASP BE DROPPIN' SCIENCE!

HAHA

WOOP!

PRODUCER, **HENRY CHALFANT** IS AMONGST THE CROWD AND GETS TO EXPERIENCE EVERY-ONE'S **REACTION** ON THE GROUND LEVEL.

BARBARA AN' EVA 62 THEY WERE GIRLS.

HA, WASP LOOK LIKE RICHARD PRYOR'S TRICK BABY!

HA!

HAW, YOU STUPID!

HAW!

SHU UP!

Shhhh...

OH, MAN! HA HA!!

HENRY AND TONY GET NEARLY **UNANIMOUS** PRAISE FROM THE VARIOUS PRINCIPAL **WILD STYLE/STYLE WARS** PLAYERS IN ATTENDANCE.

HENRY!

WASP?

MOTHERFUCKER, YOU SPENT ALL THAT TIME WITH ME... WASTED ALL THAT TIME? I'M IN THE FLICK FOR LIKE 20 SECONDS?!

I EVER SEE YOU AGAIN I'M GONNA FUCK YOU UP! I MIGHT HURT YOU **BAD !!!**

HENRY TAKES **WASP'S** THREATS SERIOUSLY...

HAI! HAI! HAI! HAI!

AS FOR THE THEATER-OWNER AT THE END OF THE OPENING...

THOSE LITTLE MUTTS EVEN TAGGED UP UNDER MY SINKS! FUCK YOU ALL! THIS AIN'T WORTH IT! ...

THROUGHOUT THE LATE '70S AND EARLY '80S **COSMO D** AND HIS CREW **JAM-ON PRODUCTIONS** OWNS THE **PARKS** AND **PLAYGROUNDS** OF BED-STUY BROOKLYN.

YESH Y'ALL!!

JAM ON IT!

YO, **COSMO**, YOU WHIPPED US THIS TIME 'ROUND, BUT I BET YOU CAN'T DO **THIS**...

WIKKI WIKKI WIKKI

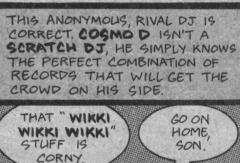

THIS ANONYMOUS, RIVAL DJ IS CORRECT. **COSMO D** ISN'T A **SCRATCH DJ**, HE SIMPLY KNOWS THE PERFECT COMBINATION OF RECORDS THAT WILL GET THE CROWD ON HIS SIDE.

THAT "WIKKI WIKKI WIKKI" STUFF IS CORNY.

GO ON HOME, SON.

IN SPITE OF HAVING A **HIP HOP/BATTLE** MENTALITY, **JAM-ON PRODUCTIONS** DOESN'T ACTUALLY THINK MUCH OF **RAP MUSIC**.

WE'LL MAKE ANTI-RAP RECORDS!

INTERESTED IN NEW, FUNKY SOUNDS, COSMO INVESTS HIS HARD-EARNED MINIMUM WAGE PAYCHECK TO PURCHASE AN **ELECTRO-HARMONIX MINI-SYNTHESIZER**.

WE'LL CALL OUR GROUP THE **POSITIVE MESSENGERS** AND MAKE SONGS TO LET PEOPLE KNOW WHAT'S GOING ON... GIVE THEM THE MESSAGE OF **JESUS**... **ALL THAT!**

WHILE PRODUCING AN **ELECTRO-FUNK** DEMO CALLED **COMPUTER AGE** ABOUT HOW DIGITAL TECHNOLOGY IS TAKING OVER, **COSMO D** IS ELATED WHEN HE HEARS THE NEW **BAMBAATAA** SONG, **PLANET ROCK**.

COSMO WANTS THE **POSITIVE MESSENGERS** DEMO TO BE RICH WITH CONTENT.

I'LL JUST FILL THIS LAST BIT OF TAPE UP WITH SOME **JOKE NONSENSE**.

JAM ON REVENGE IS THE PERFECT VENUE FOR THE **ANTI-RAP** VIBE COSMO MENTIONED EARLIER.

THESE **MUNCHKIN** VOICES IS **HYSTERICAL**!!

HE EVEN INCLUDES A STRATEGIC DISS OR TWO.

YEAH, BUT CAN YOU GUYS DO THIS? **WIKKI WIKKI WIKKI WIKKI**.

AH HA HA HA HA HA !!!!

THE GOAL WAS TO TAKE THE DEMO TO PLANET ROCK'S LABEL **TOMMY BOY** RECORDS BUT SOMEHOW PRODUCER **JOE WEBB** GETS HOLD OF THE TAPE FIRST.

NOT BAD. NOT BAD.

AS ANY CREATIVE PERSON CAN RELATE, WHEN WEBB GET TO THE END OF THE TAPE WITH **JAM ON REVENGE**, THE LAST MINUTE, JOKE TRACK...

THIS IS IT! THIS IS YOUR BIG HIT!! IT'S WORTH A **MILLION BUCKS**!!

WIKKI WIKKI WIKKI WIKKI

COSMO AND CREW AGREE TO RELEASE **JAM ON REVENGE** ON **MAYHEW RECORDS** BUT SINCE IT'S JUST A SIMPLE-MINDED PARTY RECORD, THEIR GROUP NAME **POSITIVE MESSENGERS** DOESN'T REALLY WORK. THEY CHOOSE **NEWCLEUS** BECAUSE THE GROUP IS COMPOSED OF SEVERAL FAMILIES INTO ONE CORE UNIT. THE **SCIENTIFIC** NATURE OF THE NAME CORRESPONDS NICELY WITH THEIR FUTURISTIC VIBE AND AESTHETIC.

CLUB NEGRIL...

HEY, IS THAT THE **TREACHEROUS THREE**?

HOLD TIGHT FOR A SECOND.

KOOL MOE DEE! SPECIAL K!! MY NAME'S **RICK RUBIN**. I'M A **REKKID PRODUCER...**

HILLBILLY RECORDS?

HA HA

THE STUFF YOU GUYS DID FOR **ENJOY REKKIDS** IS SOME OF MY FAVORITE RAP. **NEW RAP LANGUAGE!** FUHGETTABOUTIT...

...BUT YOUR **SUGAR HILL** REKKIDS ARE DOG SHIT. I CAN TELL YOU HATE 'EM TOO. I CAN HELP YOU GUYS MAKE THE REKKIDS YOU'RE **SUPPOSED** TO BE MAKING.

...SOMETHING **BETTER** THAN **RUN-DMC'S SUCKER MC'S!!**

MOE DEE, SPECIAL K, AND **RICK RUBIN** BUILD A FAST FRIENDSHIP. ON A DAY WHERE MOE IS FREE FROM HIS STUDIES AT **SUNY** HE MAKES THE TRIP TO RUBIN'S **NYU** DORM...

SORRY, RICK, WE'RE BOUND BY CONTRACT TO **SUGAR HILL RECORDS.**

39

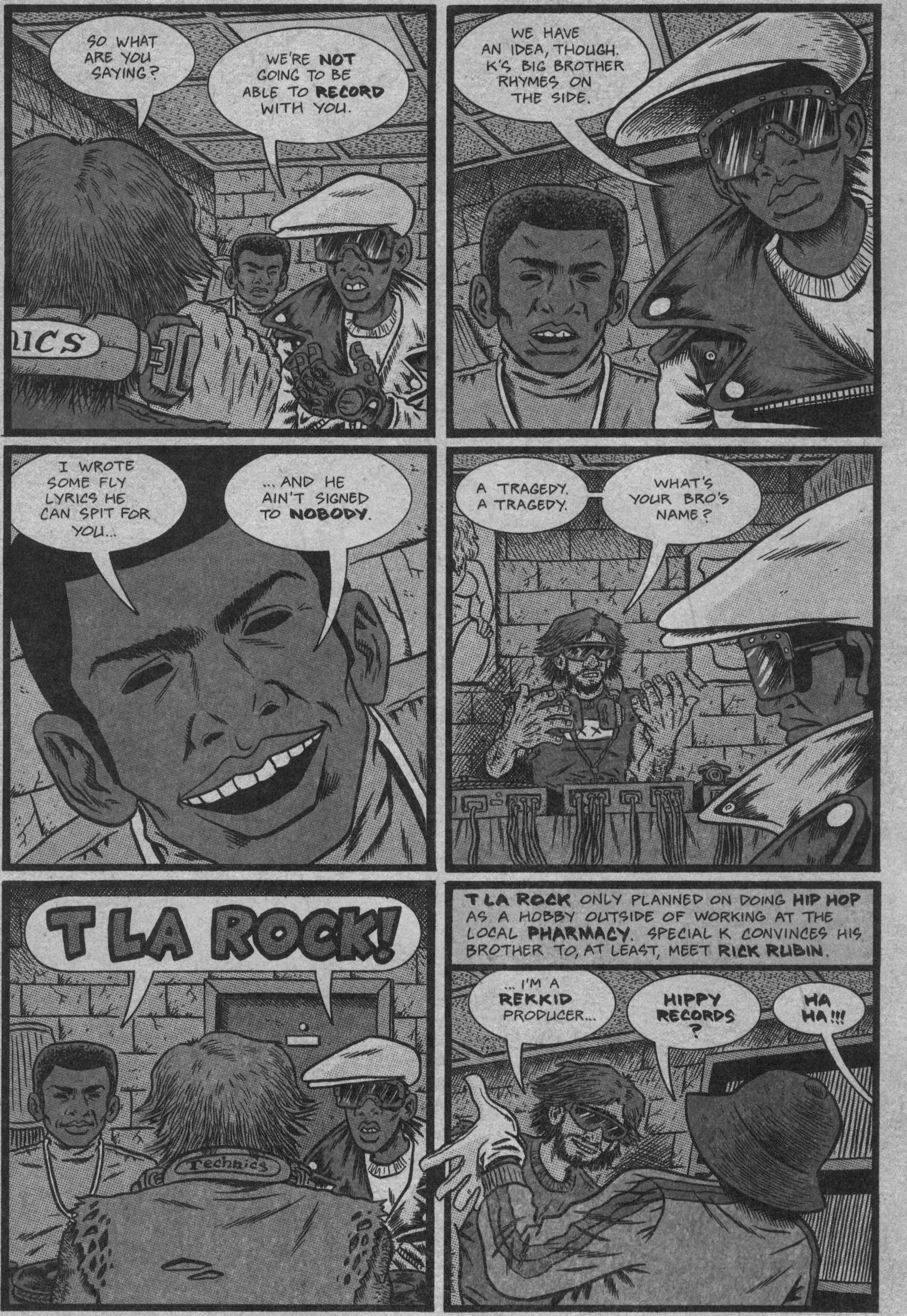
SO WHAT ARE YOU SAYING?
WE'RE **NOT** GOING TO BE ABLE TO **RECORD** WITH YOU.
ICS
WE HAVE AN IDEA, THOUGH. K'S BIG BROTHER RHYMES ON THE SIDE.
I WROTE SOME FLY LYRICS HE CAN SPIT FOR YOU...
...AND HE AIN'T SIGNED TO **NOBODY**.
A TRAGEDY. A TRAGEDY.
WHAT'S YOUR BRO'S NAME?
T LA ROCK!
Technics
T LA ROCK ONLY PLANNED ON DOING **HIP HOP** AS A HOBBY OUTSIDE OF WORKING AT THE LOCAL **PHARMACY**. SPECIAL K CONVINCES HIS BROTHER TO, AT LEAST, MEET **RICK RUBIN**.
...I'M A **REKKID** PRODUCER...
HIPPY RECORDS ?
HA HA!!!

MR. BILL STEPHNEY

YEP...

...WE'RE TRYING SOME INTERESTIN' STUFF AT THE STATION.

PROGRAM DIRECTOR WBAU-FM 90.3 ADELPHI UNIVERSITY

"EVERYBODY **SNAPPED** ON **LONG ISLAND**. CALLED US BUMPKINS BECAUSE WE HAVE GRASS YARDS IN FRONT OF OUR HOMES. THEY **BUST** ON ME FOR ATTENDING A LILY-WHITE COLLEGE. IMAGINE THAT ONE DAY I GOT LUNCH AT THE **ADELPHI** CAFETERIA AND TO MY SURPRISE..."

SPECTRUM... **MC CHUCKY D**?!!

TUNA VEGGIE HAM

HMMMM...

"**SPECTRUM CITY** IS THE HARDEST **DJ CREW** ON LONG ISLAND. WHO KNEW THAT THEIR MAIN **EMCEE** WENT TO SCHOOL HERE TOO?"

THE RADIO STATION'S A'IGHT BUT Y'ALL **DON'T** PLAY ENOUGH **RAP** MUSIC.

Y'KNOW A COUPLE JOCKS ARE GRADUATING AND A FEW SLOTS WILL BE OPEN. YOU'RE STUDYING **COMMUNICATIONS** HERE, NO?

GRAPHIC DESIGN.

"**CHUCK** STARTED CALLING SOME SPORTS GAMES FOR THE STATION. HE'D ALSO ANSWER PHONES FOR ME ON **THE MR. BILL SHOW**."

DARRYL FROM **STRONG ISLAND** ON LINE SIX.

"PRETTY SOON I GAVE THE **SPECTRUM CITY** DJS A BLOCK ON SATURDAY NIGHTS FROM 11:30-1 AM."

THE **SUPER SPECTRUM MIXX SHOW**, Y'ALL. HEAR THE DRUMMER GET **WICKED**.

CHUCKY, WE DON'T HAVE ENOUGH RECORDS TO FILL UP OUR AIRTIME.

THEN WE SHOULD START PLAYING **RECORDS** THAT WE **PRODUCE**.

HANK SHOCKLEE

"THE SHOW GAINED POPULARITY RATHER QUICKLY DESPITE THE LOW BROADCAST POWER OF OUR SIGNAL. WHENEVER WE WOULD HAVE **LIVE** EVENTS, WE COULD ALWAYS RELY ON **CHUCKY D** TO WHIP UP SOME DOPE POSTERS AN' FLYERS."

WHY HE GOTTA MAKE "FAT BOYS" BIGGER THAN OUR NAME?

"ACTUAL RAPPERS STARTED GETTING BOOKED ON THE **SUPER SPECTRUM MIXX SHOW**. THE FIRST GUY I THINK WAS..."

SPYDER D!!

"BUT, THEN..."

...GOING TO **LOS ANGELES** WAS A TRIP. IT'S LIKE A DIFFERENT **UNIVERSE** OUT THERE!

"I RECENTLY ROLLED INTO THE STUDIO AND **SPECTRUM CITY** HAD THIS **KNUCKLEHEAD** SCREENING THEIR PHONECALLS."

YEEEAAAAH, BOY! YOOO, WHATCHOO SAY YA NAME WAS AGAIN, HOMEBOY. YO YUH FROM THE 'VELT?* DIDJO MOMS GIVE ME CRABS, G? HA HA HA HA HA HA HA HA HA!!

HA HA...

* ROOSEVELT, LONG ISLAND

IMAGINE IF A CAT THIS ANIMATED HAD HIS OWN SHOW ON THESE **AIR-WAVES**?!

"COLLEGE IS A GOOD PLACE FOR **EXPERIMENTATION** SO I FIGURED 'WHAT THE HELL?' I'LL REPLACE HIM IN AN INSTANT IF I NEED TO, BUT RIGHT NOW HE'S THE **LEAD-IN** FOR THE **SUPER SPECTRUM MIXX SHOW** ON SATURDAYS."

THE MC DJ FLAVOR SHOW, BOOOOOOOY!!

WBAU-FM 90.3! GO AXE SOMEBODY IF YOU DON'T KNOW WHAT I'M SAYIN', KNOW WHAT I'M SAYIN'? HA HA AH HA HA HA HUH!!

ERIC "VIETNAM" SADLER HAD TO MOVE HIS BAND'S EQUIPMENT OUT OF HIS MOTHER'S BASEMENT TO A **PRACTICE SPACE** HE RENTED AT **510 S. FRANKLIN AVE.** IN **HEMPSTEAD.**

$200 A MONTH AIN'T BAD SO LONG AS WE PLAY ENOUGH GIGS TO JUSTIFY IT...

ERIC'S BANDMATE, **CHARLES CASSEUS,** WENT TO HIGH SCHOOL WITH **EDDIE MURPHY.** THE YOUNG COMEDIAN WOULD EVEN OPEN UP FOR THE BAND ON A REGULAR BASIS.

...WHITE FOLKS BE BELIEVING THAT **ROCKY** MOVIE IS TRUE AN' SHIT...

MURPHY HAD ALWAYS WANTED TO BE A MUSICIAN. WHEN HE GOT THE GIG ON **SATURDAY NIGHT LIVE** HE BOUGHT TONS OF STATE OF THE ART **EQUIPMENT** AND STORED IT AT SADLER'S STUDIO SPACE WHILE MOVING, FIRST CROSSTOWN, THEN TO **NEW JERSEY.**

...LONG AS THESE **BEATBOXES** ARE IN OUR POSSESSION...

...I'LL LIVE HERE 24/7!

EDDIE WAS EVEN GOING TO HAVE **SADLER** PRODUCE HIS RECORD UNTIL HIS MANAGERS STEPPED IN.

THE **DARKNESS BROTHERS** WOULDN'T COME INTO THE ABYSS WITH ME.

RICK JAMES BITCH!

ABOUT A YEAR OR SO AFTER SETTLING INTO **510 S. FRANKLIN,** ERIC SADLER GOT A SURPRISE CALL FROM **HANK SHOCKLEE,** THE INFAMOUS **SPECTRUM CITY** DJ.

OUR MOMS IS PISSED... WE RUNNIN' UP HER ELECTRIC BILL. TAKIN' UP TOO MUCH SPACE...

DON'T TRIP, MAN THERE ARE SOME OPEN ROOMS HERE AT **510.**

KEITH SHOCKLEE

WHEN **SPECTRUM CITY** GOT THEIR **RADIO SHOW** ON WBAU THEY STARTED PRODUCING DEMOS OF THEIR OWN AND FOR OTHERS AT **510.**

HA HA! PEOPLE THINK THESE ARE REAL RECORDS JUST BECAUSE THEY HEAR THEM ON THE **RADIO.**

ONE OF THE GROUPS THAT SPECTRUM RECORDED WAS CALLED THE **TOWNHOUSE THREE**...THIS TIME THEY BROUGHT ALONG A TASMANIAN DEVIL.

CHUCKY D, MEET **MC DJ FLAVOR**...

THIS KID CAN **PLAY** ANY INSTRUMENT BUT WE CAN'T FIGURE OUT WHAT TO DO WITH HIM.

EVERYBODY AGREED THAT **FLAVOR'S** PIANO RENDITION OF **CAT STEVENS' WAS DOG A DOUGHNUT** WORKED GREAT AS PART OF THE BEAT FOR THIS NEW **TOWNHOUSE THREE** DEMO.

HA HA! HE'S STUPID! HAW!

ALMOST 10 YEARS LATER THE **TOWNHOUSE THREE** CHANGE THEIR NAME TO **SON OF BAZERK** AND THEIR DEBUT ALBUM IS PRODUCED BY THE **SPECTRUM CITY** CREW NOW KNOWN AS **THE BOMB SQUAD.**

RK

OF

...AND **FLAVOR** STUCK WITH **MC CHUCKY D** AND GANG EVER SINCE...

WHAT TH... **FLAVOR** !!!!

YO, G! IT WASN'T MY FAULT, G! I THOUGHT I SAW A MOUSE, YO! MEESES TO PIECES, YOU KNOW'M SAYIN' G? HA HA HA... YA FEEL ME, RIGHT? HA...

BEING A CRATE DIGGER, **HANK SHOCKLEE** HAS BUILT **FRIENDSHIPS** WITH MANY RECORD STORE EMPLOYEES. ONE OF THEM HAS OFFERED A SHOT TO ACTUALLY MAKE A RECORD.

HMMM... I'LL **ASK** THE FELLAS BUT WE'RE REALLY **RADIO DJS** MORE THAN **RAP PERFORMERS**.

HOW MUCH THESE COST?

ONE CONDITION FROM **VANGUARD** RECORDS IS THAT **PINKY VALEZQUEZ** WILL HAVE TO PRODUCE THE **SPECTRUM CITY** RECORD ON THE STRENGTH OF HIS RECENT HIT **ELECTRIC KINGDOM** BY **TWILIGHT 22**.

THIS ISN'T THE KINDA BEAT WE WOULDA MADE...

TOO FAST... OH WELL...

MC CHUCKY D AND HIS HYPE-MAN **BUTCH CASSIDY** ARE THE PRINCIPLE EMCEES. THEIR FIRST TRACK IS A POIGNANT JAM CALLED **LIES**.

THE DEAL IS TO TRUST AND NOT TO **DESPISE**!!

BUTCH GETS EXTRA WORK AS AN EDDIE MURPHY IMPERSONATOR.

THE PROOF IS IN THE PUDDING IF YOU JUST **REALIZE**.

HAVING A LITTLE MORE STUDIO TIME BOOKED, **SPECTRUM CITY** RECORDS **CHECK OUT THE RADIO** WITH INFLUENCE FROM THE **SHOCKLEE** BROTHERS AND **ERIC "VIETNAM" SADLER**.

WHY NOT MAKE A JAM ABOUT THE **RADIO STATION**?

NEITHER TRACK CAUSES MUCH OF A STIR, BUT **CHECK OUT THE RADIO** IS A FAVORITE OF MANY HIP HOPPERS ONCE THEY HEAR THE TUNE BROADCAST ON **WBAU-FM 90.3**.

IN 1992, **CHECK OUT THE RADIO** WAS REVISITED AFTER ALMOST 10 YEARS IN THE FEATURE FILM, **SOUTH CENTRAL**.

DEUCE, HERE!

THE PRAGMATIC **CHUCKY D** HELPED **FLAVOR** GET A JOB WITH HIM DELIVERING FURNITURE FOR HIS FATHER'S BUSINESS BY DAY.

...SO, I'LL BE LIKE: "SUCKERS TO THE SIDE I KNOW YOU HATE MY 98." AN' YOU'LL BE LIKE...

YOU'RE GONNA GET YOURS!

SPECTRUM CITY SPENDS THEIR NIGHTS PLAYING SHOWS AND PARTIES TO TRY AND PROMOTE THEIR RECORD'S RELEASE. **CHUCKY D'S** VISIBILITY BECOMES A **TARGET.**

YO, CHUCK! THEY OUT TO GET US, MAN!!

...THIS BROTHER FROM THE "PLAY HARD CREW" STOPPED ME AN' AXED ME "WHAT'S UP WITH THAT BROTHER CHUCKY D? HE SWEARS HE'S NICE!"

I SAID "CHUCKY D DON'T SWEAR HE'S NICE. HE KNOWS HE'S NICE."

I GOT THE FEELING YOU'RE TURNING INTO A PUBLIC ENEMY, G. DUDES IS JEALOUS AND OVER OVER-ZEALOUS, G!!

SPECTRUM CITY IMMEDIATELY HEADS TO **510 S. FRANKLIN** TO RECORD A **BATTLE RECORD** TO PUNK-DOWN THEIR HATERS. REPURPOSING **BLOW YOUR HEAD** BY **FRED WESLEY** AND THE **JB'S, PUBLIC ENEMY NUMBER ONE** SPINS IN REGULAR ROTATION ON **ADELPHI** COLLEGE RADIO, ESPECIALLY ON **DOCTOR DRE'S** SHOW, **THE OPERATING ROOM.**

'CUZ I CAN GO SOLO LIKE A SUGAR RAY BOLO...

COINCIDENTALLY, **RUN DMC** WAS IN STUDIO ONCE WHILE THE RECORD WAS BOOMING **CHUCKY D'S** VOICE OVER THE AIRWAVES.

DRÉ, IMMA NEEDA **TAPE** OF THIS JOINT.

AIN'T NO THANG, JMJ.

IN **1984**, HIP HOP IS STILL **STRONGEST** IN THE STREETS SO IT'S NO SURPRISE TO SEE **RAP CYPHERS** IN THE HOMELESS SHELTERS AND GROUP HOMES OF **NEW YORK CITY.**

BOMP!

KRISHNA, COME GET UP IN THIS.

!

LAWRENCE PARKER IS AMONGST THESE MASSES BUT HIS INQUISITIVE NATURE COMPELS HIM TO STUDY WITH THE **HARE KRISHNAS** WHO PASS FOOD TO THOSE IN NEED AT THE SHELTER.

...MMMMMMMMMMMMMMMMMMMMM...

DON'T GET **CONFUSED**. RAP AND EMCEEING ARE STILL IMPORTANT TO PARKER THOUGH HE INSTANTLY BECOMES INTRIGUED BY **GRAFFITI CULTURE** ONCE HE MEETS CERTAIN PEOPLE AT THE HOME.

YOU'RE **ZORE**? I SEE YOUR NAME **EVERYWHERE**!! I THOUGHT **ZORE** WAS A GANG OF **DUDES.**

YOUR DRAWINGS IS NICE. I'LL TAKE YOU OUT **BOMBING** NEX' TIME I GO.

THESE LAY-UPS IS A PERFECT PLACE TO **PRACTICE,** KRISHNA.

MY NAME'S **LARRY!**

WHAT NAME YOU GONNA WRITE, ANYWAY?

UMM...

HURRY UP, **KRISHNA,** THEY'RE GON' START SERVIN' BREAKFAST AT THE **HOME.**

ALMOST THERE...

As LAWRENCE gets more and more serious with PAINTING GRAFFITI he becomes aware of the work that's already out there...

Parker makes moves to spruce up his handle, KRS in a strong authoritative way and the nomenclature persists over nearly everyone.

AFTER **T LA ROCK** AND HIS LITTLE BROTHER **SPECIAL K** WORK TOGETHER ON SOME LYRICS THEY HEAD OVER TO **RICK RUBIN'S** DORM.

SOUND PLUS RHYTHM DONE UP WITH **FINESSE**...

...IS EQUIVALENT TO THE ADJECTIVE "**BEST**"...

NOW IT'S TIME TO INTRODUCE...

...NEO-**RHYMES COMBINED** TO THE GROOVE WITH **JUICE**...

ADAM HOROVITZ

ADAM YAUCH

MICHAEL DIAMOND

T LA ROCK BRINGS HIS DJ, **LOUIE LOU**, ALONG BUT AN ARGUMENT BREAKS OUT OVER WHO GETS TO BORROW RUBIN'S **SCRATCH TRACK** FOR PRACTICE. T WANTS TO PERFECT HIS RHYMES, **LOUIE LOU** WANTS TO ADD HIS OWN TOUCHES ON THE **TURNTABLE**.

FUCK Y'ALL!

RICK RUBIN CONVINCES HIS FAVORITE DJ, **JAZZY JAY** TO BE THE MAN ON THE WHEELS OF STEEL.

YOU DON'T HAVE TO AXE ME TWICE TO GET IN A STUDIO. WHAT HAPPEN WIT' OUR **SEX PISTOLS** REMIX, THOUGH?

WHEN **T LA ROCK** AND **JAZZY JAY** ARE CONFIDENT WITH THEIR PARTS OF THE PERFORMANCE, **RICK** BRINGS EVERYBODY TO **POWER PLAY STUDIO**, THE SAME PLACE RUBIN PRODUCED RECORDS FOR HIS BAND **HOSE**.*

T-L-A-R-O-C-K...

...USUALLY THE REASON FOR A VERY NICE **DAY**...

* AS SEEN IN HHFT vol.2 -- ENERGETIC ED

AS AN ASIDE, THIS IS WHERE **JAZZY JAY** INTRODUCES THE **BEASTIES** TO ONE OF HIS FAVORITE **BEVERAGES**.

BRASS MONKEY!!

MMM...

WHEN THE TIME COMES, **ADROCK** AND FRIENDS CHIME IN FOR THE **CROWD PARTICIPATION** PART OF **IT'S YOURS**, THE **T LA ROCK** RECORD.

HOO!

HOOO!

RICK WAS GOING TO RELEASE **IT'S YOURS** ON HIS OWN UNTIL **SPECIAL K** INTRODUCES HIM TO **PLANET ROCK** PRODUCER, **ARTHUR BAKER**. BAKER AND K KNOW EACH OTHER FROM A MOVIE SET THEY'RE WORKING ON.

...SO ALL I DID WAS JUST PUT 'IM **AWAY**...

...CUZ MY G.I. JOE LOOKED **G.I. GAY**...

RUBIN AGREES TO SIGN **IT'S YOURS** TO ARTHUR BAKER'S **STREETWISE/PARTYTIME** LABEL TO RELEASE THE RECORD BUT INSISTS THAT HIS **DEF JAM** LOGO BE ADDED TO THE COVER.

I **Def Jam** recordings

RICK RUBIN'S DORM ADDRESS →

AVIS

DEF JAM RECORDINGS, 5 UNIVERSITY PL. NEW YORK, N.Y. 10003, (212) 420-8666

RECORDING **IT'S YOURS** WAS A FUN EXPERIENCE FOR **T LA ROCK** BUT HE HAS NO DELUSIONS.

TERRY, GOT ANOTHER ONE FOR YOU TO DELIVER. SLIGHTLY UPTOWN.

COMMENTATING, ILLUSTRATING, DESCRIPTION GIVING...

!

MR. LEROY, THIS IS MY RECORD ON THE RADIO!!

I'LL NEED YOU TO SWEEP UP A FEW THINGS WHEN YOU GET BACK, TERRY.

...ADJECTIVE EXPERT...

RUSSELL "RUSH" SIMMONS MANAGES ALL THE STRONGEST RAP ACTS OF THE DAY AND HE'S INCREDIBLY INTRIGUED BY THIS MYSTERIOUS **T LA ROCK** RECORD THAT'S CONSTANTLY PLAYING ON THE RADIO.

GET ME **RED ALERT** ON THE LINE...

...I WANNA KNOW THE **NIGGA'TH** WHO MADE THITH REKKID...

DOUG E. FRESH SPENT A LOT OF TIME BUILDING HIS REPUTATION IN **NEW YORK** HOPING FOR A SHOT AT MAKING RECORDS. HE ACCOMPLISHES THIS **MULTIPLE** TIMES...

TURNS OUT THOSE EXPERIENCES DIDN'T REALLY GO AS **DOUG E. FRESH** WOULD HAVE HOPED...

THESE **PRODUCERS**... THEY ALL JERK YOU **CREATIVELY**...

RECORD LABEL OWNERS ALL JERK YOU WHEN IT'S TIME TO GET **PAID**!

FROM NOW ON I'MMA HAVE'TA HAVE MORE SAY IN THE THINGS I MAKE.

HE MAY NOT BE HAPPY WITH THE RESULTING RECORD DRAMA BUT ONE THING IS CLEAR: HE'S **WELL-ESTABLISHED** WITHIN THE **HIP HOP** COMMUNITY. AT LEAST ENOUGH TO JUDGE SOME LOCAL TALENT SHOWS.

I WAS WALKIN' THROUGH THE **HALLS**, SCRATCHIN' MY **BALLS**, MY DICK GOT CAUGHT IN THE **ELEVATOR WALL**...

...MY LADY **SCREAMED**, MY DICK TURNT **GREEN**, AN' THAT'S THE END OF MY **DING-A-LING**...

NEXT!

AN EVENT AT **170TH ST.** AND **JEROME**...

...I'D LIKE TO ENTER IN THIS **RAP CONTEST** YOU'RE HAVING, SIR.

WE GOTTA SPOT OPEN. WHAT YOU SAY YOUR NAME WAS, AGAIN?

MC RICKY D...

RICKY D'S STRONG CHARACTERISTICS OF **STORYTELLING** AND **HUMOR** EARNS HIM THE TOP SPOT AT THE SHOWCASE WITH A CASH PRIZE OF **$1500**.

...HE OPENED IT UP WITH HIS BARE TWO **THUMBS**...

...HE SEEN CRABS WITH **SPEARS AND INDIAN DRUMS**!!

MORE IMPORTANTLY, **DOUG E. FRESH** AND **MC RICKY D** MEET AFTER THE CONTEST, BECOME FRIENDS, AND START BUILDING **ROUTINES** TOGETHER...

YOUR WIFE: SHE DON'T LIKE SEX **A LOT**. TO-DAY SHE'S READY AND...

HOT HOT HOT!

IN FACT, **DOUG E. FRESH** AND **MC RICKY D** RAPIDLY BECOME **UNDERGROUND** STARS ONCE **BOOTLEG TAPES** OF THEIR EARLIEST LIVE PERFORMANCES SPREAD AROUND **NEW YORK CITY**. FRESH OUT OF THE GATE THESE FIRST ROUTINES WILL BECOME THE BACKBONE OF BOTH THEIR CAREERS FOR **DECADES** TO COME ONCE **DOUG** AND **RICK** COMMIT THEIR TALENT TO **WAX**.

..THERE'S GIRLIES OUT HERE THAT SEEM **APPEALIN'**...

..BUT, THEY'LL COME IN YOUR LIFE AN' COLD HURT YOUR **FEELIN'S**...

...I'M TELLIN' YOU... AS **RICK** IS MY **NAME**...

...I WOULDN'T TRUST NO GIRL UNLESS SHE FEELS THE **SAME**...

LA-DI-DA-DI, WE LIKES TO **PAW-TEE**, WE DON'T CAUSE TROUBLE, WE DON'T BOTHER **NOBODY**...

...WE'RE **JUSSUMEN** THAT'S ON THE **MIC**, AND WHEN WE ROCK UP ON THE **MIC** WE ROCK THE **MIC**...

RIGHT!

HEY, YO **DOUG**, PUT YUH BALLY'S **ONNN**...

WHAT?

I WAS ABOUT TO BUT I NEED A **SHOEHORN**...

WHY?

...BECAUSE, THESE SHOES ALWAYS HURT MY **CORNS**...

...6 MINUTES... ...6 MINUTES... ...6 MINUTES DOUG E. FRESH YER ON...

53

IF YOU GET HOLD OF ONE OF THESE TAPES YOU'LL DISCOVER A **LEGENDARY** 1984 BIT THAT **NEVER** TRANSITIONED TO RECORDS (PROBABLY FOR SLANDER REASONS).

SHE DIDN'T HEAR CUZ I SAID IT KINDA **LOW**. HE DIDN'T HEAR CUZ I SAID IT KINDA **LOW**... AN' THEN I BROKE OUT BECAUSE I REALLY HAD TO **GO**.

I SAW **MISS AMERICA**... SHE GOT **MILLIONS**... I'M TALKIN' 'BOUT THAT THAT HO NAMED **VANESSA WILLIAMS**...

YO, SHE SAW **ME, MC RICKY D**... SHE CAME UP CLOSE AN' SHE GRABBED MY **BODY**, SHE SAID...

...HOLD ME, HOLD ME, NEVER LET ME GO UNTIL YOU TOLD ME, TOLD ME...

... I SAID " **UM**, LISTEN **UP** YA DUMB **SLUT**... CHECK YOUR FINGER- NAILS FROM OFF MY **BUTT**..."

"... AND ON SECOND THOUGHT YOU LOOK NICE IN THAT **LEATHER**" STILL QUITE SHOCKED I SAID " WELL, I'D **NEVER**..."

..." I THINK YOUR FINGERS ARE A LITTLE TOO **STICKY**." SHE SAID " OH, **RICKY**, I THINK YOU'RE TOO **PICKY**..."

...I SAID "ME PICKY? **HELL NO!**" SO I TOOK OFF MY PANTS AN' TOLD HER TO...

"**SWING LOW!**"

CHARLIE STETTLER TO SAL ABBATIELLO

...BUT, THE **DISCO THREE** REALLY HAVE A SHOT IF I COULD JUST GET THEM A GOOD **PRODUCER**.

I'LL TALK TO HIM BUT I AIN'T MAKIN' NO **PROMISES**...

SAL ABBATIELLO TO KURTIS BLOW

...INTRIGUING. I GOTTA THINK ABOUT IT, THOUGH.

KURTIS BLOW TO HIS MANAGER **RUSSELL "RUSH" SIMMONS**

I DON'T KNOW... THEM **FAT** MUTHA-FUCKA'TH ITH **CO'NY.**

AFTER DELIBERATION, **KURTIS BLOW** HELPS THE **DISCO THREE** CREATE A NEW BRAND BY PRODUCING THEIR RECORD **FAT BOYS.**

FAT BOYS!

YOU KNOW THEY'RE DOWN BY LAW...

FAT BOYS!

THEY GIVIN' YOU MUCH MUCH MORE...

THE SINGLE SELLS **100,000** UNITS IN 4 AND A HALF WEEKS...

I'M TH'TILL TH'KEPTICAL...

THE RECORD IS SO POPULAR, IN FACT, THAT **STETTLER** HOLDS A **SPECIAL EVENT** AT THE **ROSELAND BALLROOM** FOR THE **DISCO THREE.**

...YOUR NAMES ARE OFFICIALLY NOW THE **FAT BOYS!**

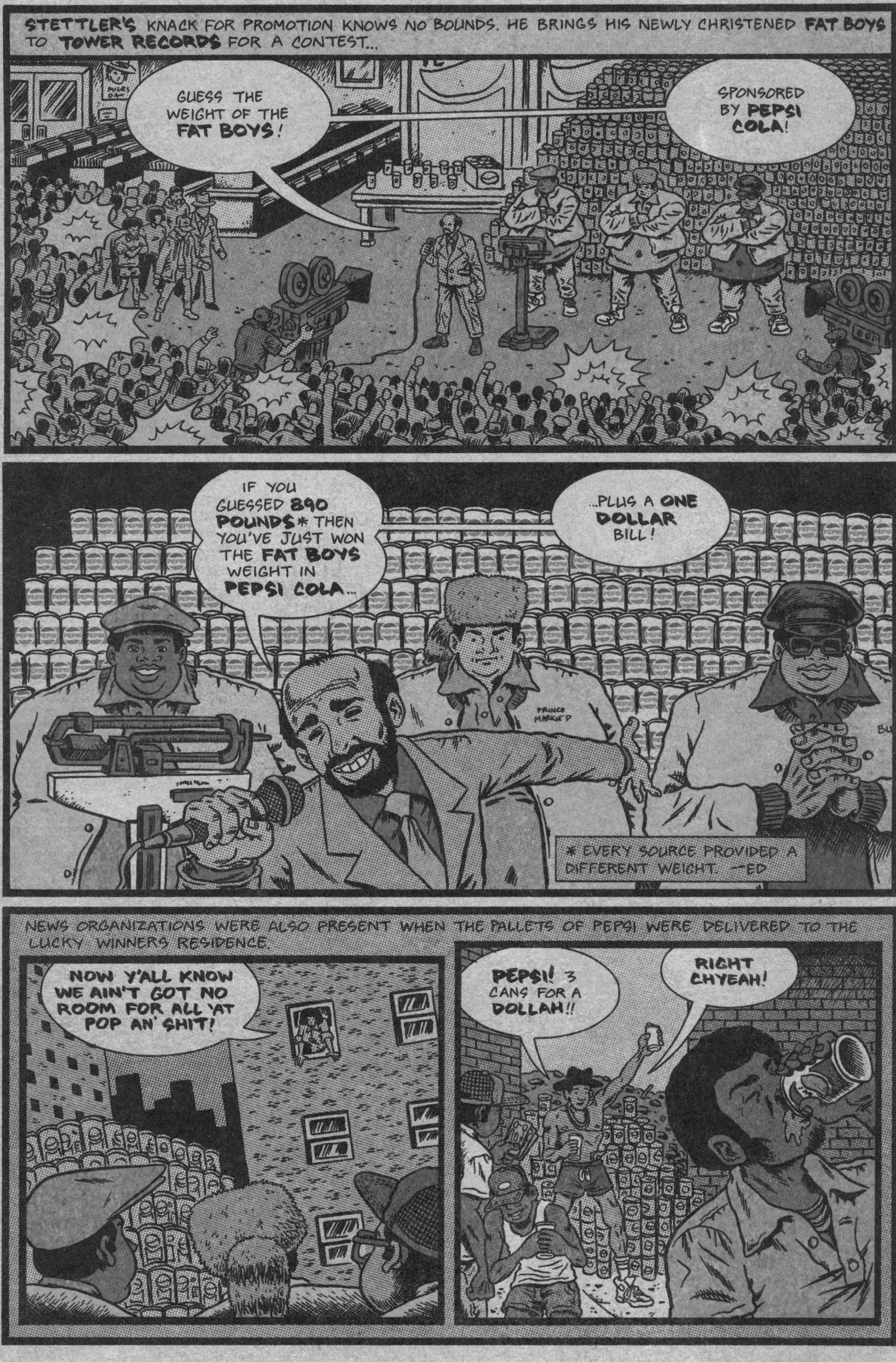

STETTLER'S KNACK FOR PROMOTION KNOWS NO BOUNDS. HE BRINGS HIS NEWLY CHRISTENED FAT BOYS TO TOWER RECORDS FOR A CONTEST...
GUESS THE WEIGHT OF THE FAT BOYS!
SPONSORED BY PEPSI COLA!
IF YOU GUESSED 890 POUNDS* THEN YOU'VE JUST WON THE FAT BOYS WEIGHT IN PEPSI COLA...
...PLUS A ONE DOLLAR BILL!
* EVERY SOURCE PROVIDED A DIFFERENT WEIGHT. —ED
NEWS ORGANIZATIONS WERE ALSO PRESENT WHEN THE PALLETS OF PEPSI WERE DELIVERED TO THE LUCKY WINNERS RESIDENCE.
NOW Y'ALL KNOW WE AIN'T GOT NO ROOM FOR ALL 'AT POP AN' SHIT!
PEPSI! 3 CANS FOR A DOLLAH!!
RIGHT CHYEAH!

RUN DMC WERE PROTESTING THEIR PRODUCER LARRY SMITH HAVING HIS FRIEND, SESSION-PLAYER EDDIE MARTINEZ, LAY SOME HEAVY GUITAR CHORDS ON THEIR NEW RECORD. THEY SOON GIVE IN, HOWEVER, AND ROCK BOX IS BORN.

LARRY SMITH'S FUSION OF ROCK AND RAP PROVES TO BE ONE STEP IN THE RIGHT DIRECTION.

BECAUSE Y'ALL DEMAND THE BES'! HERE'S ANOTHER KOOL RED ALERT SURE-SHOT!!

AFTER A SERIES OF HIT SINGLES WITH RUN DMC, PROFILE RECORDS INFORMS RUSH ABOUT A STIPULATION IN THE CONTRACT ALLOWING THE LABEL TO CONSTRUCT AN ALBUM WHETHER SIMMONS LIKES IT OR NOT.

BATH'TIDTH...

FIVE SOLID RECORDS IN THE CAN, **RUN DMC** ROUNDS OUT THEIR **SELF-TITLED** ALBUM WITH 4 MORE STRONG TRACKS.

PLAYLIST
1. HARD TIMES (BRALOWER, MOORE, R.SIMMONS, SMITH, WARING)
2. ROCK BOX (McDANIELS, J.SIMMONS, SMITH)
3. JAM-MASTER JAY (McDANIELS, MIZELL, J & R SIMMONS, SMITH)
4. HOLLIS CREW (McDANIELS, J.SIMMONS, MIZELL)
5. SUCKER MC'S (N.S. HARDY, McDANIELS, J.SIMMONS, SMITH)
6. IT'S LIKE THAT (McDANIELS, J.SIMMONS, SMITH)
7. WAKE UP (J.SIMMONS, SMITH, R.SIMMONS, HAYDEN)
8. 30 DAYS (D.SIMMONS, SMITH, MOORE)
9. JAY'S GAME (J.SIMMONS, SMITH, MIZELL, R.SIMMONS)

...AND IF YOU FIND YOU DON'T LIKE MY **WAYS**...

...WELL, YOU CAN SEND ME BACK IN **30 DAYS**.

AROUND THIS TIME A SEASONED FREELANCE MUSIC WRITER NAMED **BILL ADLER** BEGINS WORKING FOR **RUSSELL SIMMONS** OUT OF SHEER ENTHUSIASM FOR THIS YOUNG ART FORM.

WHAT CAN I DO FOR YOU AND HOW MUCH CAN YOU PAY?

I DON'T KNOW... AND **NOTHING**.

ADLER SPOTS A HOLE IN **RUSH PRODUCTIONS'** BUSINESS PLAN: **PUBLICITY**. ADLER'S NEVER BEEN A PUBLICIST, BUT HE'S ALWAYS DEALT WITH THEM DURING HIS DECADE OF JOURNALISM.

LOOK, RUSS, WE HAVE **POSITIVE** REVIEWS OF THE **RUN-DMC** ALBUM.

ROLLING STONE, CREEM, THE VILLAGE VOICE!!

THE **RUN DMC** ALBUM EXPONENTIALLY OUTSELLS ITSELF EACH WEEK AS **HUNDREDS OF THOUSANDS** FLY OFF THE SHELVES, DROPPING A **MASSIVE** AMOUNT OF CASH IN THE LAPS OF THE SMALL **PROFILE RECORDS** LABEL, WHO ARE EAGER TO REINVEST.

YEAH, THOUND'TH GOOD. I'LL LET THE BOY'TH KNOW.

THO THE COMPANY WANT'TH TO MAKE A MYOO'THICK VIDEO FOR Y'ALL.

FOR WHAT SONG?

ROCK BAWK'TH...

AW, MAN...

EVERYBODY GONNA MAKE FUN A THEM **GUITARS**.

IT TOOK AN EMBARRASSINGLY LONG TIME FOR BLACK MUSICIANS TO APPEAR ON **MTV**. YOU MIGHT CATCH A SPORADIC VIDEO HERE OR THERE...

IT REALLY WASN'T UNTIL **MICHAEL JACKSON'S THRILLER** VIDEO BECAME A SMASH HIT BLOCKBUSTER THAT **MTV** AND THEIR CORPORATE OVERSEERS FELT COMFORTABLE ENOUGH TO ALLOW SOME **COLOR** INTO REGULAR ROTATION.

OLA RAY, PLAYMATE OF THE MONTH, JUNE 1980

THE LAST **RAP** VIDEO ON MTV AT THIS POINT WAS **RAPTURE** BY **BLONDIE** WHICH APPEARED THE FIRST DAY OF THE CHANNEL'S BROADCAST.

...SURE SHOT...

THE FEW EXISTING RAP VIDEOS OF THE DAY WOULD ONLY APPEAR ON LOCAL, SYNDICATED NYC SHOWS LIKE **VIDEO MUSIC BOX** AND **NEW YORK HOT TRACKS**.

FOREVER IN A **WORLD** OF YOU AND A **GIRL**... A FEW GRAMS IN A PIPE TO MAKE YOUR HEAD **SWIRL**...

YOU MUST SPREAD THE WORD OF THE **MASTER TEACHA** OR **DIE** BY THE **RHYMES** AND THE STREETS'LL **EAT CHA.**

"STEP OFF" BY GRAND-MASTER MELLE MEL

RUN DMC'S **ROCK BOX** VIDEO WAS FINELY SCULPTED FOR **MTV**'S CONSIDERATION. THE FAMILIAR FACE OF COMEDIAN **PROFESSOR IRWIN COREY** INTRODUCES RAP AND RUN-DMC TO THE SHELTERED HOME VIEWER.

NOW WHAT IS A **FUGUE**...

A **FUGUE** IS LIKE A RAP...

EDDIE MARTINEZ'S GUITAR PLAYING JUXTAPOSED WITH **RUN DMC**'S PERFORMANCE IS AKIN TO THE TEAM-UP OF **EDDIE VAN HALEN** AND **MICHAEL JACKSON** ON **BEAT IT**.

THE MIXED CROWD OF **BLACK** AND **WHITE** DANCERS ALONGSIDE **RUN DMC** AT THE **PUNK** VENUE **DANCETERIA** WAS NOT AN ACCIDENT.

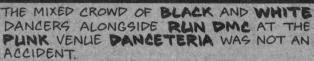

NOR WAS THE BRIEF, NON-VERBAL EXCHANGE BETWEEN **JAM MASTER JAY** AND THE KID.

WINK!

WINK!

THE **ROCK BOX** VIDEO IS AN AMAZING BRIDGE THAT CONVINCINGLY SELLS THE IDEA OF THE **RAP-ROCK STAR** BUT **RUN DMC** MANAGES TO INVADE **MTV** WITHOUT EVEN SLIGHTLY COMPROMISING THEIR CORE **HIP HOP** VALUES.

OUR DJ IS BETTER THAN ALL THESE BANDS!!

PROFILE RECORDS' **$27,000** GAMBIT PAYS OFF AS **MTV** FOLDS **ROCK BOX** INTO REGULAR ROTATION, WHICH INCREASES RECORD SALES, AND KEEPS THE NETWORK OPEN TO RUNNING MORE RAP VIDEOS IN THE FUTURE.

TWENNTY THEVVEN GEE'TH FOR THE VIDEO!!!

THEY ONLY GAVE UTH A $25,000 **ADVANT'TH** TO MAKE THE FUCKIN' REKKID!!

USING HIS EXISTING DEMO REEL, **MICHAEL HOLMAN** IS ABLE TO SECURE A TOTAL BUDGET OF $150,000 FROM INDEPENDENT INVESTORS FOR HIS **SOUL TRAIN**-INSPIRED **HIP HOP** TELEVISION SHOW. HE RECRUITS GRAFFITI ARTIST **BRIM FUENTES** TO HELP DRESS THE SET AND COME UP WITH A FLY LOGO.

ORIGINALLY THE HOPE WAS TO HAVE EITHER **FAB FIVE FREDDY** OR **MR. MAGIC** FILL THE **DON CORNELIUS** ROLE BUT THEY LACKED AVAILABILITY WHEN IT CAME TIME TO SHOOT SO **HOLMAN** STEPPED INTO THE SLOT.

SO DON'T TOUCH THE DIAL, THERE IS NO **WAY**...

...CUZ **GRAFFITI ROCK** IS HERE TO **STAY**...

KOOL MOE DEE AND SPECIAL K OF THE TREACHEROUS THREE ARE THE INTRODUCTORY EMCEES ON THE **GRAFFITI ROCK** PILOT. **LA SUNSHINE**, THE THIRD MEMBER, OF THE GROUP DIDN'T PARTICIPATE DUE TO **DRUG** ISSUES.

IF YOU NEVER SAW A BREAKER DO A HEAD-SPIN...

... THEN, CHECK OUT THIS!

AFRIKA BAMBAATAA, AS MUSICAL CONSULTANT, SUGGESTS **DJ JIMMY JAZ** TO MIX THE RECORDS THAT EVERYBODY WOULD BE DANCING TO.

DON'T TRY IT AT HOME WITH YOUR DAD'S STEREO...

ONLY UNDER **HIP HOP** SUPERVISION.

HOLMAN'S FRIEND AND BANDMATE **VINCE GALLO** WAS RESPONSIBLE FOR ACCUMULATING THESE DANCERS. THE INVESTORS SURELY CHIMED IN WITH THEIR TWO CENTS WHEN VETTING THE PARTICIPANTS.

WE **WON'T** BE ABLE TO SELL THE SHOW IF YOU DON'T SPRINKLE SOME **WHITE** FACES IN THE CROWD.

TOO MANY **BLACKS** AND **PUERTO RICANS** WILL SCARE OFF THE POTENTIAL ADVERTISER MARKET, YOU UNDERSTAND?

VINCE GALLO EVEN GETS A LITTLE SCREEN TIME TO SHINE FOR HIS TROUBLES.

...PRINCE VINCE!

ANOTHER HIP CITY-KID WHO POPS UP IS DEBI MAZAR, YEARS BEFORE HER ACTING CAREER BEGAN.

THE NEW YORK CITY BREAKERS, A GROUP CREATED AND MANAGED BY MICHAEL HOLMAN WAS SCHEDULED TO DO A FEATURE NUMBER... AND THEN A REP FROM THE SCREEN ACTORS GUILD SHOWED UP TO DEMAND MORE MONEY FOR THE BOYS.

THIS IS BULLSHIT!

THE NEGOTIATIONS GO NOWHERE AND THE BREAKERS HIT THE STUDIO TO DO WHAT THEY DO BEST.

PULLING OUT ALL THE STOPS TO MAKE A BIG SPLASH WITH THIS FIRST EPISODE, MICHAEL HOLMAN CALLS A FAVOR IN TO RUSSELL SIMMONS TO SECURE RUN DMC FOR A PERFORMANCE OF SUCKER MC'S

FIRST COME...

...FIRST SERVED BASIS...

THE **RUN DMC** PIECE SEGUES INTO A FAUX RAP BATTLE WITH THE TWO MEMBERS OF THE **TREACHEROUS THREE**.

SO I THINK I'M JUST GONNA BACK OUT!

WORD!

IT GETS SET OFF WITH STRONG, RIGID, B-BOY AUTHORITY.

RUN'S FREESTYLE LYRICS END UP ON WAX IN THE FUTURE.

MOE DEE'S PARTNER ADDS A PLAYFUL ENERGY TO THIS MOCK EXHIBITION.

DMC WOULDN'T LET YOU FORGET HIS NAME IF YOU TRIED.

...'CAUSE WHEN IT COMES TO RAP, I'M THE **EPITOME**... THE RAPPERS **IDOL** AND MY **TITLE** IS **KOOL MOE DEE.**

THEY CALL ME **ILLER** THAN **ILLER**. THERE'S NO ONE **CHILLER**. IT'S NOT MICHAEL JACKSON AND THIS IS NOT **THRILLER**.

WELL I'M ONE OF THE CHOSEN **FEW**. SO WHEN YOU NEED A LIFT JUST TO GET YOU **THROUGH**... ALL YOU HAVE TO DO IS **SAY** SPECIAL **K.**

WELL, I'M **DMC** IN THE PLACE TO BE... AND THE PLACE TO **BE** IS WITH **DMC**...

THE MCS TRADE VERSES BACK AND FORTH A FEW TIMES AND GLARINGLY AVOID DIRECT COMBAT EACH TIME.

WELL DON'T TOUCH THAT DIAL, JUST SIT **TIGHT**.

IF YOU LIKED THAT "BATTLE"... **HA!** THAT WAS **LIGHT**.

I KNOW YOU'RE GONNA LOVE THIS NEXT **ACT**...

'CUZ WE'LL HAVE **SHANNON** WHEN WE GET **BACK**...

ON AN EPISODE OF THE DOCUMENTARY TELEVISION SERIES **UNSUNG**, **KOOL MOE DEE** REVEALS SOME BEHIND THE SCENES SCOOP ON THE **GRAFFITI ROCK** BATTLE.

HEY, **MOE DEE**. CAN I RAP TO Y'ALL A MINUTE?

WHAT'S UP, **JMJ**?

YOU KNOW MY DUDES, **RUN DMC**, ARE NEW, RIGHT? YOU **CAN'T** DO THEM LIKE YOU DID **BUSY BEE STARSKI*** A'IGHT??!

* HHFT vol.1 -- EL EDUARDO

HEY, IF THEY DON'T COME AT US THEN I WON'T **SMOKE** 'EM.

THAT'S FAIR.

THE **PILOT** IS SYNDICATED IN **88** DIFFERENT MARKETS NATIONWIDE AND HITS PRESENT AND FUTURE HIP-HOPPERS LIKE A TON OF BRICKS.

FAB FIVE FREDDY

THIS SHOW IS THE **BLUE-PRINT**.

THE BEASTIE BOYS

...HA HA HA HA HA...

MINDBLOWING !!!!

Q-TIP (AGE 14)

YOU KNOW, SON, THIS RE-MINDS ME OF BEBOP.

WHEN IT CAME TIME TO SHOP **GRAFFITI ROCK** AROUND AS A SERIES, **MICHAEL HOLMAN** HIT A DOMINO-EFFECT OF TELEVISION EXECUTIVES WITH **COLD FEET**.

CHICAGO

IF **LOS ANGELES** PICKS UP THE SHOW THEN IT'LL BE A **NO-BRAINER** FOR US.

LOS ANGELES

...ONLY WAY WE'D FEEL COMFORTABLE BUYING THE SERIES WOULD BE IF **NEW YORK** HAS FAITH ENOUGH TO JUMP IN AS WELL.

NEW YORK CITY

WHAT'S IT WORTH TO YOU, COCK-SUCKER??

GRAFFITI ROCK DIDN'T CATCH FIRE THE WAY MICHAEL HOLMAN WOULD HAVE HOPED, BUT THE SHOW HAD A VERY SIGNIFICANT IMPACT ON HIP HOP THANKS TO THE WELL-ATTENDED AFTERPARTY.

GIRLS!

DOUBLE R! ME AND YAUCH WILL BE OVER THERE.

JAZZY JAY!

YO!

WHO IS THAT?

RUSSELL "RUSH"...

RUSSELL SIMMONS? SHUT UP! HIS NAME'S ON EVERY RAP REKKID THAT MATTERS!

YOU DON'T KNOW 'IM? HE COOL. I'LL INTRODUCE Y'ALL.

HEY, RUSH. MEET MY MAN, RICK RUBIN.

WE MADE THAT IT'S YOURS REKKID TO- GETHER.

NOW, HOW THE FUCK DID A WHITE BOY MAKE MY FAVORITE RAP REKKID OUT RIGHT NOW?

AIN'T THAT ABOUT A BITCH!

AFTER A NIGHT OF CONVERSATION IT BECOMES CLEAR THAT **RICK** AND **RUSSELL** ARE OPERATING ON SIMILAR WAVELENGTHS. A FRIENDSHIP DEVELOPS.

WE HAVEN'T SEEN A **DIME** YET FROM **IT'S YOURS.** NOT SURE IF WE'RE BEING **JERKED** BY THE LABEL OR NOT.

I WONDER IF YOU CAN MAKE HEADS OR TAILS OF IT? YOU MUST GET GOOD DEALS FOR YOUR GUYS. **RUN DMC** ALONE...

RUN DM THEE? ITH YOU TH'MOKIN'? WE GETTIN' JERKED JUTH'T THE THAME. AIN'T MADE TOO MUCH BEYOND OUR ADVANT'TH.

MONEY ISN'T THE MOST IMPORTANT THING BUT HOW THE HELL CAN WE AT LEAST BREAK EVEN?

RUSH HELPS OUT BY SIGNING RICK'S MC **T LA ROCK** TO A MANAGEMENT DEAL, WHICH GETS MORE LIVE GIGS AND MEANS MORE MONEY IN THE POCKET.

ONE DAY AT RICK'S DORM...

YEAH, I STILL WANNA MAKE MORE RAP REKKIDS.

BEEN MAKING TRACKS IN MY SPARE TIME. GREAT EMCEE'S ARE HARD TO COME BY...

COWBELL! CLAP! CLAP!

HOLY FUCK!! YOU COULD PUT ANY RAPPAH OVUH THEETH TRACK'TH AND THEY'LL BE HIT REKKID'TH! HOW MANY BEAT'TH DO YOU GOT, RICK?

I DON'T KNOW, 50?

LARRY-LAIR, WE GIVE IN TO YOU A LOT, BUT **NOT** THIS TIME.

IT SOUND TOO R & B FOR OUR TASTE.

THE BOY'TH AW RIGHT IN THITH CAYTH, LARRY...

THITH BEAT OF YOUR'TH WOULD BE PERFECT FOR THEM NEW DUDE'TH, THOUGH...

WHAT'TH THEIR NAME'TH? **HOUDINI**?

"WHODINI"

SICK WIT' IT!

YO, LARRY! WE IN BIDNIZ, MAN.

THE TRACKS THAT **LARRY SMITH** HAS BEEN SITTING ON DO PLENTY TO CONVINCE **JIVE RECORDS** THAT HE'S THE GUY WHO SHOULD BE PRODUCING MUSIC FOR **WHODINI**.

WHAT'TH UP, **TOKYO ROW'TH**. WHATCHOO DOIN' LATER?

RUSSELL, RUSSELL...

ANN CARLI, JIVE RECORDS A & R

HIS **MATURITY** AND **EXPERIENCE** IS JUST WHAT THE GROUP NEEDS TO ARTICULATE THEIR IDEAS TO THE **BRITISH** SESSION PLAYERS.

NOT BAD, BUT MORE LIKE THIS, MAN.

YOU NOTICE THAT WHENEVER LARRY'S INTO THE JAM HE'S ALWAYS GRABBIN' ON HIS **JOHNSON**?

"WELL, WE SPENT **TWO WEEKS** MAKIN' THE REKKID AND HE DIDN'T TAKE HIS HAND OFF HIS JOINT ONCE."

FRIENDS!

HOW MANY OF US HAVE THEM?

ESCAPE IS THE CLASSIC, SECOND RECORD BY WHODINI, RELEASED ON OCTOBER 17, 1984. IT RAPIDLY BECOMES ONE OF RAP MUSICS FIRST PLATINUM ALBUMS.

YOU GOT A BIG MOUTH!

WHODINI ESCAPE PLAYLIST

1. FIVE MINUTES OF FUNK
2. FREAKS COME OUT AT NIGHT
3. FEATURING GRANDMASTER DEE
4. BIG MOUTH
5. ESCAPE (I NEED A BREAK)
6. FRIENDS
7. OUT OF CONTROL
8. WE ARE WHODINI

GRANDMASTER DEE
(IF YOU PLEASE)

SUPER-LISTENER GRANDMASTER DEE FROM LONG ISLAND IS A SCRATCH DJ WHO FREQUENTLY CALLS THE MR. MAGIC RADIO SHOW.

NEW YORK'S GONNA KEEP HEARING MY NAME UNTIL SOMEONE PUTS ME ON.

JALIL AND ECSTASY WERE IN NEED OF A GREAT DJ FOR THEIR LIVE PERFORMANCES. MAGIC MENTIONS DEE TO HIS FORMER INTERN, JALIL.

DEE, I'VE HEARD ENOUGH.

THE REST IS HISTORY...

KURTIS BLOW'S WIFE HAS A STROKE OF GENIUS...

BASKETBALL IS THE NUMBER ONE SPORT WITH BRUTHA'S BUT **NONE** OF Y'ALL MADE A RAP RECORD ABOUT IT YET...

YOU RIGHT.

WITH STRONG LABEL APPROVAL KURTIS PUTS HIS FRIEND **BILLY BILL** TO WORK TO WRITE SOME LYRICS...

I WANT ALL THE **LEGENDS** IN THIS JAM...

...BUT **DR. J** HAS TO BE THE FIRST DUDE MENTIONED...

BASKETBALL GETS HUGE RADIO-PLAY AND THE **50,000** COPIES OF THE **KURTIS BLOW** SINGLE QUICKLY VANISH. THE SONG IS FEATURED ON HIS 1984 ALBUM, **EGO TRIP**, AND HELPS THE RECORD GO **GOLD**.

BASKETBALL IS MY FAVORITE **SPORT**...

...I LIKE THE WAY THEY DRIBBLE UP AND DOWN THE **COURT**...

BASKETBALL'S SUDDEN POPULARITY CONVINCED **MERCURY/POLYGRAM RECORDS** TO SCRAPE $25,000 TOGETHER TO MAKE A **MUSIC VIDEO**.

...I GET IT, BUT WHY DO WE GOTTA HAVE NINJAS AND GIANT CHICKENS AND NON-SENSE IN THE VIDEO?

THE IDEA IS TO CAPTURE THE SPIRIT OF ALL THE BIG INFLUENCES IN THE **BRONX**.

ON THE ROAD, KURTIS CAUGHT HELL FOR HAVING ALL WHITE CHEERLEADERS IN THE VID

HMPHRPH...

MY BRUTHA. WE MUST SPEAK...

KURTIS HAD A ONCE IN A LIFETIME OPPORTUNITY AND MADE SURE TO GET SOME OF HIS FRIENDS INTO THE VIDEO.

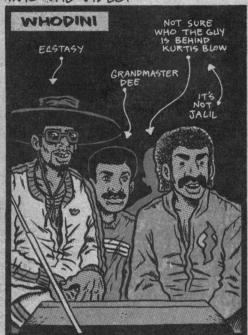

WHODINI

ECSTASY

GRANDMASTER DEE

NOT SURE WHO THE GUY IS BEHIND KURTIS BLOW

IT'S NOT JALIL

THE FAT BOYS

WHEN THE SONG REALLY CATCHES FIRE THE **NBA** BEGINS SHUTTLING **KURTIS** AROUND THE COUNTRY TO BOOST ATTENDANCE AT GAMES IN LAGGING MARKETS.

BAS-KET BALLLLL...

WE LOVE THAT BAS-KET BALLLLLL!

SIDENOTE: TWO OTHER SONGS FROM **KURTIS BLOW'S EGO TRIP** ALBUM ARE WORTH NOTING...

8 MILLION STORIES...

SHE'S MORE SINISTER THAN **PETER LORRE** AND THIS IS JUST TWO OF...

...EIGHT MILLION STORIES...

AJ SCRATCH*

THAT'S RIGHT, CH'YALL...

...HIS NAME IS AJ...

* NOTEWORTHY FOR BEING RIFE WITH SAMPLE FODDER AND IT'S REVERANCE TO THE DJ.

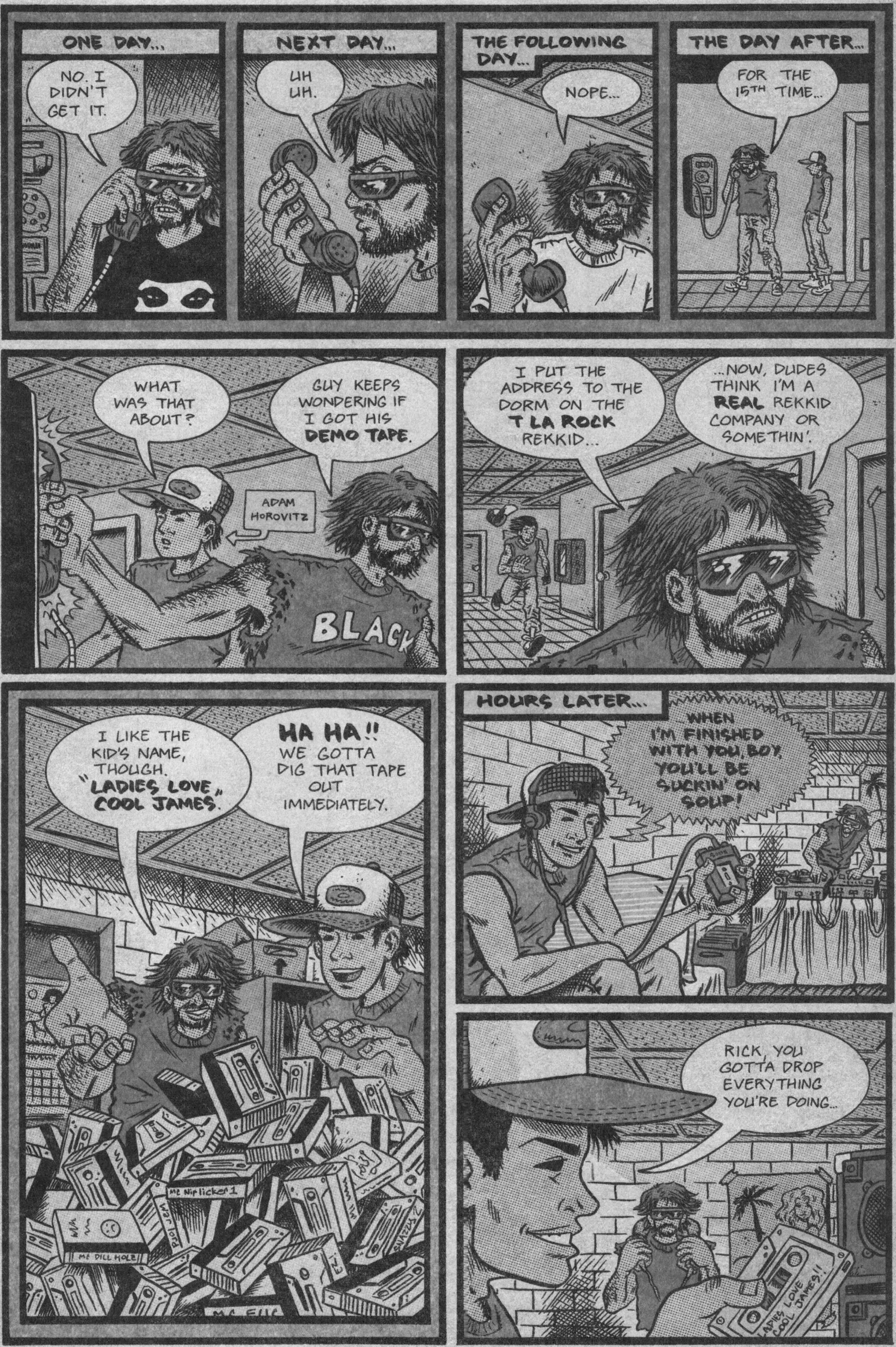
ONE DAY...
NO. I DIDN'T GET IT.
NEXT DAY...
UH UH.
THE FOLLOWING DAY...
NOPE...
THE DAY AFTER...
FOR THE 15TH TIME...
WHAT WAS THAT ABOUT?
GUY KEEPS WONDERING IF I GOT HIS **DEMO TAPE**.
ADAM HOROVITZ
BLACK
I PUT THE ADDRESS TO THE DORM ON THE **T LA ROCK** REKKID...
...NOW, DUDES THINK I'M A **REAL** REKKID COMPANY OR SOMETHIN'.
I LIKE THE KID'S NAME, THOUGH. "**LADIES LOVE COOL JAMES**."
HA HA!! WE GOTTA DIG THAT TAPE OUT IMMEDIATELY.
HOURS LATER...
WHEN I'M FINISHED WITH YOU, BOY, YOU'LL BE SUCKIN' ON SOUP!
RICK, YOU GOTTA DROP EVERYTHING YOU'RE DOING...

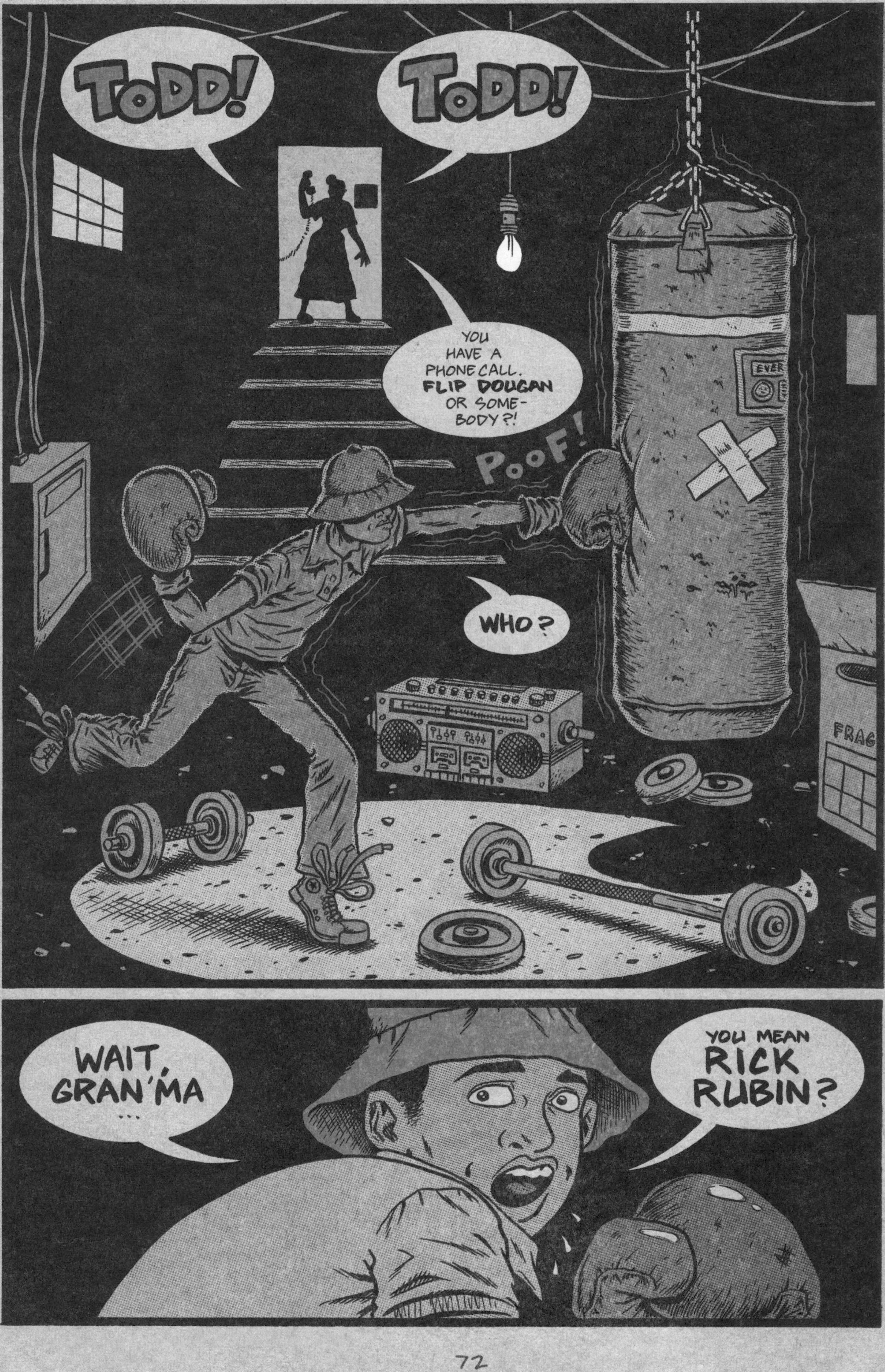
TODD!
TODD!
YOU HAVE A PHONE CALL. FLIP DOUGAN OR SOME-BODY?!
POOF!
WHO?
WAIT, GRAN'MA ...
YOU MEAN RICK RUBIN?

NAME: RUSSELL "RUSH" SIMMONS
OCCUPATION: MANAGER
LOCATION: NEW YORK CITY

NAME: LYOR COHEN
OCCUPATION: BANK ANALYST
LOCATION: LOS ANGELES

I PRAWMITH YOU'LL NEVVUH GET **RUN DM THEE** FOR A CHEAPAH PRYTH THAN THITH...

IT WILL BE GREAT. GET THE BOYS OUT HERE IN TWO WEEKS...

LYOR IS INSPIRED TO PROMOTE RAP SHOWS AFTER ATTENDING SOME **UNCLE JAMM'S ARMY** HIP HOP PARTIES AT THE **SPORTS ARENA.**

MY NAME IS **ICE T**...

...L.A. IS WHERE I RESIDE...

HIS SPIN IS TO TRY AND PUT AN EVENT IN A PART OF TOWN MORE COMFORTABLE FOR **WHITES.**

AFTER BORROWING **$700** FROM HIS FOLKS, LYOR RENTS A **PUNK** CLUB FOR A NIGHT.

PLEASURE DOING BUSINESS...

YES!

THE **PUNK/HIP HOP** CROWD ISN'T KNOWN FOR PRE-ORDERING THEIR TICKETS. IN THE DAYS LEADING UP TO THE EVENT...

IF NOBODY SHOWS UP...

...I'M ROYALLY FUCKED..

THE NIGHT OF THE SHOW...

THE SHOWBILL FOR THE EVENING...

RED HOT CHILI PEPPERS	ICE T	FISHBONE	RUN-DMC

ALL TOLD, **LYOR** TAKES HOME **$35,000** FOR THE EVENING AFTER PAYING THE BANDS AND THE VENUE...

RUSSELL "**RUSH**", MY MAN! I TOLD YOU THE SHOW WAS GOING TO BE GREAT!

THE BOYTH ARE VERY HAPPY.

Sniff...

THERE'S GOTTA BE A FOLLOW-UP GIG. WHO DO YOU HAVE FOR ME?

WHODINI.

UNFORTUNATELY FOR LYOR HE WASN'T ABLE TO REPLICATE THE SUCCESS OF THE **RUN-DMC** SHOW...

DON'T WORRY, BOYS. I PROMISE YOU'LL STILL BE **PAID**.

ROYALLY FUCKED...

RUSH, I... DON'T KNOW WHAT HAPPENED. I LOST EVERYTHING. **EVERYTHING**. I DON'T HAVE A DIME, NOW.

I CAN TELL YOU HUNGRY AN' YOU GOT GOOD HUTH'L. WANNA COME TO **NEW YORK** AN' HELP OUT AT **RUSH MANAGEMENT**?

74

The New York City **Bureau of Child Welfare** performs the service of educating the town's homeless youth. **KRS-One** wants to be an artist so the organization foots the bill to send him to the **School of Visual Arts** in Manhattan.

No doubt this will pass, brutha.

Let's roll, Krishna!

We got about two more hours 'til we hit the fields upstate. How much are we s'posed to haul back to the city?

There's like three big-ass bundles waiting for us, man.

Doo Doo Doo Doo!

Maryyyy Jayyyy Ayyyne!

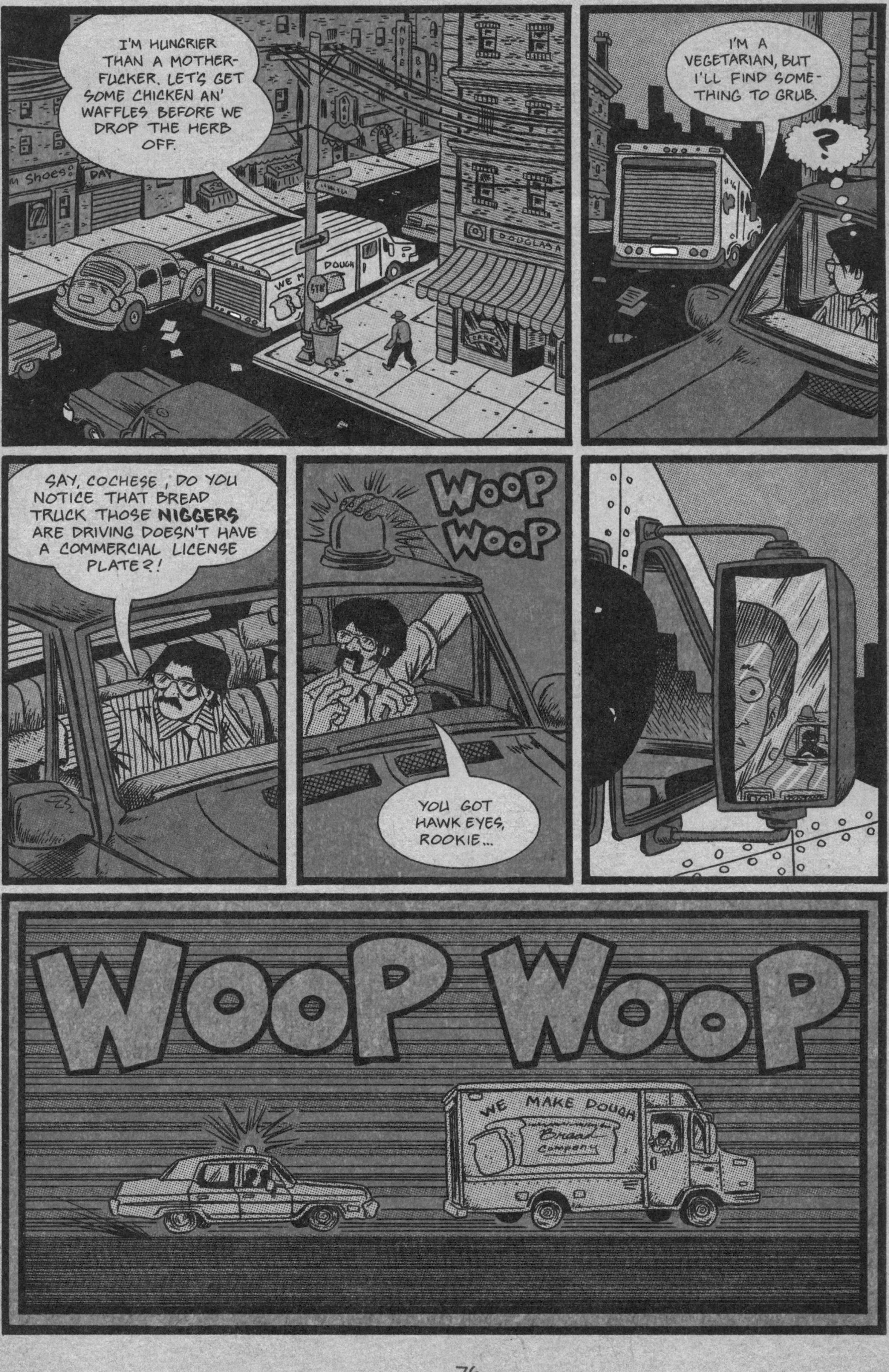
I'M HUNGRIER THAN A MOTHER-FUCKER. LET'S GET SOME CHICKEN AN' WAFFLES BEFORE WE DROP THE HERB OFF.
I'M A VEGETARIAN, BUT I'LL FIND SOME-THING TO GRUB.
?
SAY, COCHESE, DO YOU NOTICE THAT BREAD TRUCK THOSE **NIGGERS** ARE DRIVING DOESN'T HAVE A COMMERCIAL LICENSE PLATE?!
WOOP WOOP
YOU GOT HAWK EYES, ROOKIE...
WOOP WOOP
WE MAKE DOUGH
Bread Company

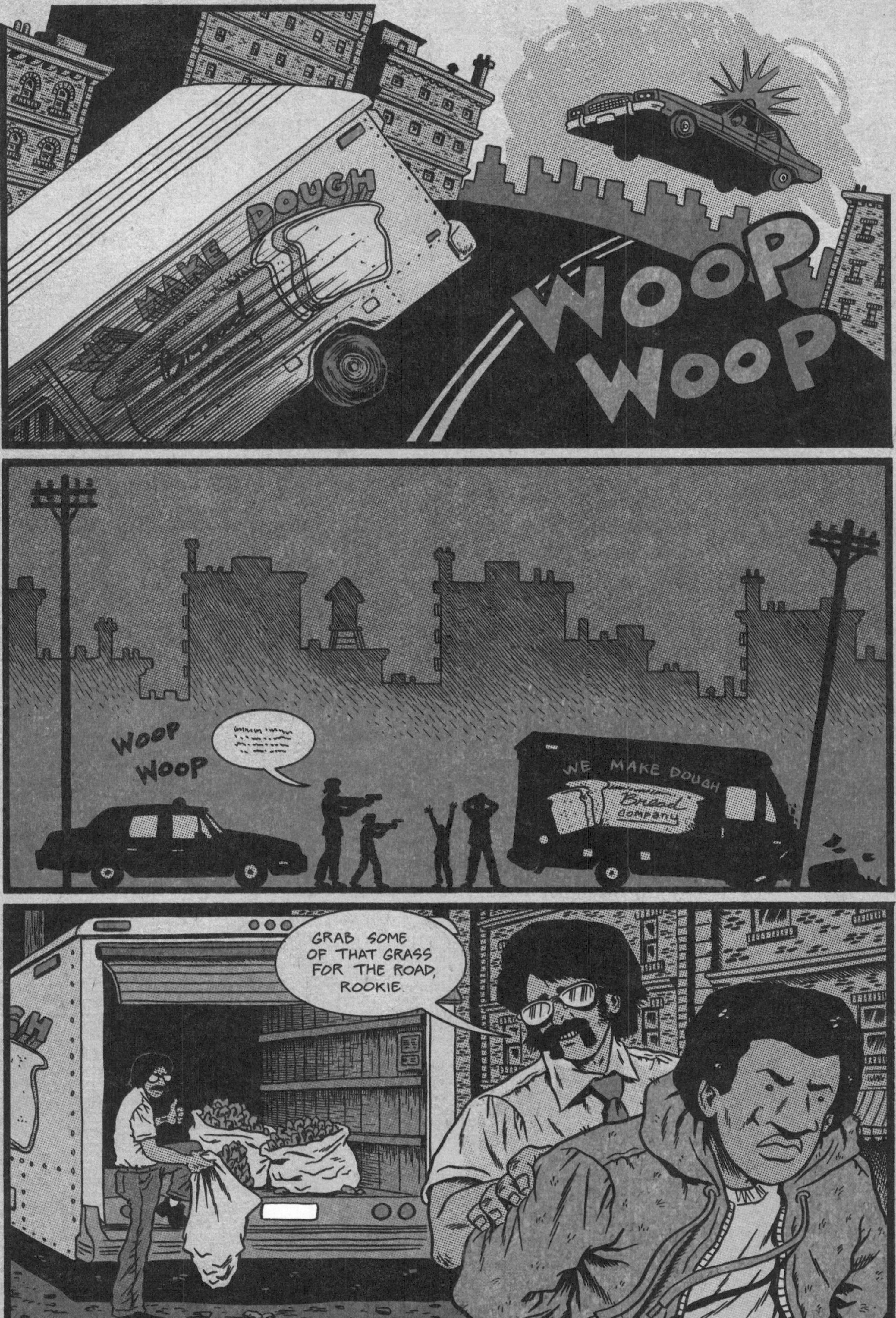
WE MAKE DOUGH
WOOP
WOOP
WOOP
WOOP
WE MAKE DOUGH
Bread company
GRAB SOME OF THAT GRASS FOR THE ROAD, ROOKIE.

THE THING I HATE ABOUT PINCHIN' YA IS ALLA DAMN PAPER-WORK. SO GIVE IT TO ME, BOY...

WHAT'S YOUR NAME? WHERE DO YA STAY?

KRISHNA PARKER.

AGE 19.

I STAY IN THE NYC.

TELL ME THE EXACT ADDRESS, BOY!!

...ISH ...HOMELESS MEN'S SHELTER, SIR...

THAT SHELTER'S FOR **MEN**, BOY. GOTTA BE 21 TO BE IN THERE. WHERE'S YER **MAMA** AT, BOY? YOU'RE EITHER GOING WITH HER OR IT'S OFF TO THE **BOYS HOME**.

MY MOMMA IS THE SUN AN' THE MOON AN' THE EARF, OFFICER...

OH, YOU'RE ONE A THEM CUTE ONES.

CAUGHT RED-HANDED, **KRS-ONE'S** FIRST OFFENSE EARNS HIM **60 DAYS** IN THE **BRONX HOUSE OF DETENTION**.

I'M NEVER COMIN' BACK TO THIS MOTHERFUCKER...

NYU DORMITORY, WEINSTEIN HALL, ROOM 712...

KNOK NOK

WHERE **RICK RUBIN** AT?

I'M RICK RUBIN...

YEAH? I THOUGHT YOU WAS A **BLACK DUDE**?

COOL!

ANYWAY... I GOT **RHYMES** BY THE **NOTEBOOK** FULL, YA KNOW WHAT I'M SAYIN'?

HMMM... WELL LET'S SEE IF WE CAN MAKE A **SONG** OUT OF ALL YOUR WORK.

"MY PAL, **ADAM**, OVER HERE HAS BEEN PROGRAMMING SOME BEATS FOR YOU TO RHYME TO."

ANOTHER WHITE BOY?

DAMN...

HA!

ADAM HOROVITZ

AN INSURMOUNTABLE BEAT SUBJECT OF **DISCUSSION**...

YOU'RE MOTIVATED BY THE AID OF **PERCUSSION**...

CUT! MORE ENERGY, LL.

THERE'S NO CATEGORY... FOR THIS STORY... IT WILL ROCK IN ANY TERRITORY...

I NEED A BEAT BY LL COOL J ...

WHAT WOULD YOU DO WITH THIS REKKID, RUSSELL?

THOUND'TH GREAT. WE COULD THEE IF PROFILE REKKID'TH WANT'TH TO FUCK WIT' IT.

BUT, YOU'RE ALWAYS COMPLAINING ABOUT ALL THESE REKKID COMPANIES. "PROFILE DOESN'T GIVE YOU WHAT YOU DESERVE." BLAH BLAH...

WHAT IF WE WORK TOGETHER AND PUT THE REKKID OUT OURSELVES?

YOU KNOW I'M WORKIN' TOWARD HAVIN' MY OWN IMPRINT AT MERCURY RIGHT? "RUSH REKKID'TH..."

THIS LL COOL J REKKID WON'T DISTURB THAT DEAL AT ALL, RUSSELL. THIS IS A SEPARATE THING.

PUT IN SOME TOKEN AMOUNT TO MAKE IT OFFICIAL. MY FOLKS WILL KICK IN A FEW GRAND. I'LL DO ALL THE WORK. JUST BE MY PARTNER...

WHAT'TH THO TH'PECIAL ABOUT ME, THOUGH, RICK?

YOU HAVE CHARM AND SWAGGER. YOUR NAME IS ON ALL THE BEST RAP REKKIDS. I'M OPERATING OUT OF A DORM AN' YOU HAVE AN ACTUAL OFFICE. YOU'LL BRING AN INSTANT LEGITIMACY TO THE OPERATION.

I'LL HAVE MY LAWYER PUT TOGETHER A PARTNERSHIP AGREEMENT...

RICK, WHO ITH THITH LITTLE CORNY **MUTHAFUCKA** AN' WHY DUH'TH HE GOT THAT OKEY-DOKE GRIN ON HITH JIB?

THIS IS **LL COOL J**, RUSSELL. HE'S GONNA BE OUR FIRST **DEF JAM** SUPERSTAR.

ARTISTIC LICENSE

NOT LOOKIN' LIKE THAT **SUGARHILL** GAW-BITCH HE AIN'T. WHERE ITH YOU FROM, YOUNG'UN?

ST. ALBANS, QUEENS...

HEY, RUSSELL, YOU SEE THIS? INSTEAD OF PUTTING "**PRO-DUCED** BY RICK RUBIN" IT READS "**RE-DUCED** BY RICK RUBIN." SUCKER MC'S WAS MY INSPIRATION.

WE NEED TO **RE-DOOTH** THITH BOYTH GET-UP.

THEE. THITH ITH WHAT I'M TALKIN' 'BOUT. IT'TH MORE REALER. NIGGA'TH WANT RAPPAH'TH TO BE LEGIT.

THIS FEELS BASIC, **RUSH**, MAN...

RICK RUBIN AGONIZES DAY AND NIGHT COMING UP WITH THE DESIGN AESTHETIC FOR THE **DEF JAM** RECORD SLEEVES AS THEIR FIRST RELEASE, **I NEED A BEAT** BY LL **COOL J**, IS IMPENDING.

WHICH MAROON SWATCH DO YOU LIKE BEST, **LYOR**?

THEY BOTH LOOK THE SAME TO ME.

ONCE THE RECORDS GET MANUFACTURED, RICK SPENDS HIS DAYS COURTING RADIO DJ'S.

FROM THE PEOPLE WHO BROUGHT Y'ALL **T LA ROCK** COMES A DUDE WHO SOUNDS LIKE T LA ROCK!

CHUCKY D

AT NIGHT HE RUBS SHOULDERS WITH CLUB DJS TO POPULARIZE THE **LL COOL J** RECORD.

...MY FUNKY POETRY...

...I'M IMPROVING THE CONDITIONS OF THE RAP INDUSTRY...

T LA ROCK?

THE LEGWORK PAYS OFF. WITHIN A FEW MONTHS **I NEED A BEAT** SELLS **100,000** UNITS FROM RICK RUBIN'S DORM ROOM.

...DON'T THWET IT.

RUSSELL, WE'RE SELLIN' REKKIDS WE DON'T EVEN HAVE. WE MIGHT NEED **HELP**!!

LADIES LOVE... LEGEND IN LEATHER...

LL COOL J

I'M NOT GONNA SING...

...BECAUSE I JUST WON'T DO THAT...

RUN DMC! I LOVE, Y'ALL!!

YO! **T LA ROCK**!! I'M LL COOL J! YOU HEAR MY RECORD YET? I SOUN' JUS' LIKE YOU!!!

YEAH...

I HEARD...

DR. JECKYLL AN' **MR. HYDE**! HEY YO, YUH REKKIDS IS **FIRE**! DO Y'ALL GOT A **MILLION** DOLLARS, YET?

I KNOW Y'ALL IS GETTIN' PAID!!!

WHAT KINDA **GIRLS** DO Y'ALL BE GETTIN'? WHAT'S YOUR **CARS** LIKE??

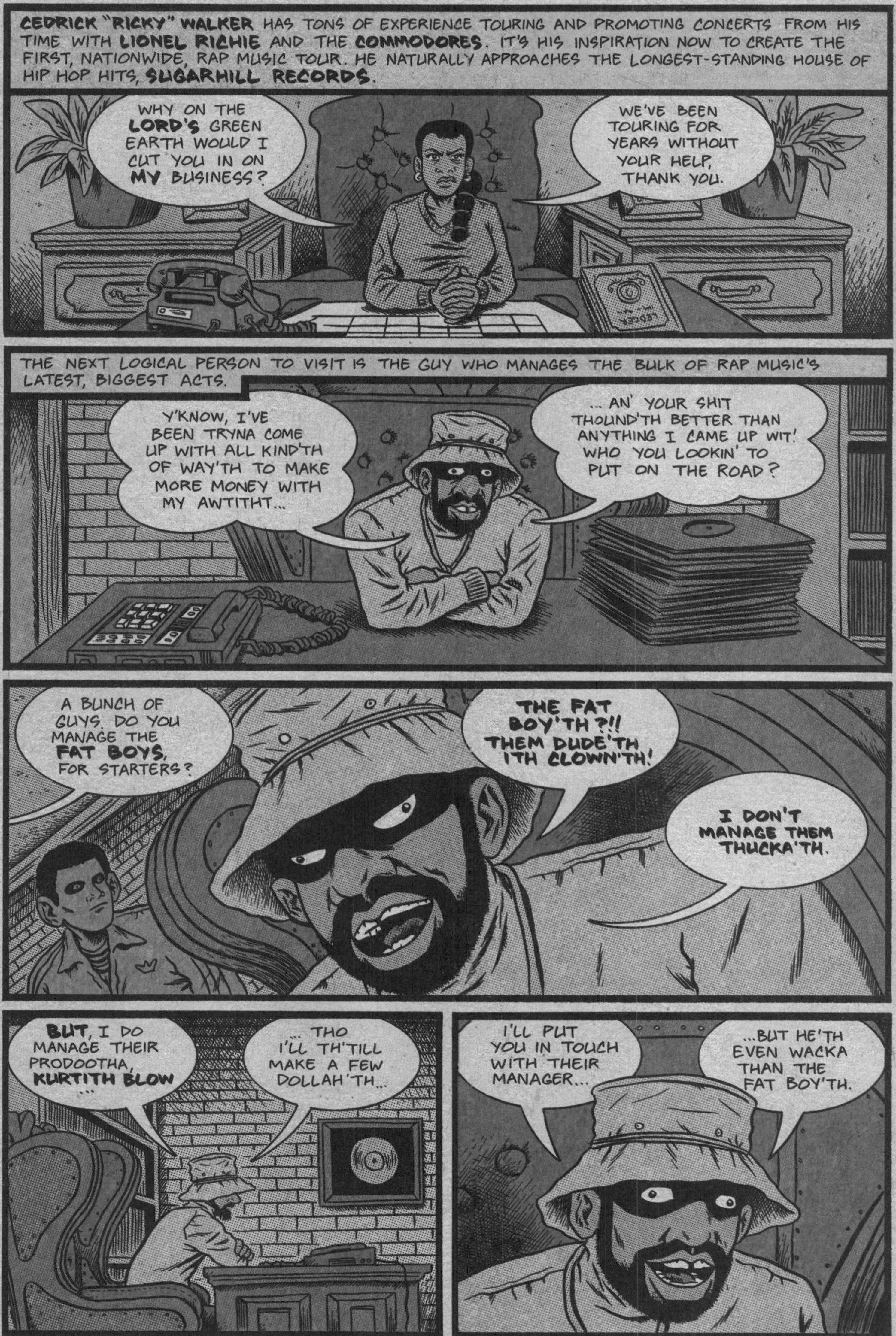
CEDRICK "RICKY" WALKER HAS TONS OF EXPERIENCE TOURING AND PROMOTING CONCERTS FROM HIS TIME WITH LIONEL RICHIE AND THE COMMODORES. IT'S HIS INSPIRATION NOW TO CREATE THE FIRST, NATIONWIDE, RAP MUSIC TOUR. HE NATURALLY APPROACHES THE LONGEST-STANDING HOUSE OF HIP HOP HITS, SUGARHILL RECORDS.
WHY ON THE LORD'S GREEN EARTH WOULD I CUT YOU IN ON MY BUSINESS?
WE'VE BEEN TOURING FOR YEARS WITHOUT YOUR HELP, THANK YOU.
THE NEXT LOGICAL PERSON TO VISIT IS THE GUY WHO MANAGES THE BULK OF RAP MUSIC'S LATEST, BIGGEST ACTS.
Y'KNOW, I'VE BEEN TRYNA COME UP WITH ALL KIND'TH OF WAY'TH TO MAKE MORE MONEY WITH MY AWTITHT...
... AN' YOUR SHIT THOUND'TH BETTER THAN ANYTHING I CAME UP WIT! WHO YOU LOOKIN' TO PUT ON THE ROAD?
A BUNCH OF GUYS. DO YOU MANAGE THE FAT BOYS, FOR STARTERS?
THE FAT BOY'TH?!! THEM DUDE'TH ITH CLOWN'TH!
I DON'T MANAGE THEM THUCKA'TH.
BUT, I DO MANAGE THEIR PRODOOTHA, KURTITH BLOW ...
... THO I'LL TH'TILL MAKE A FEW DOLLAH'TH...
I'LL PUT YOU IN TOUCH WITH THEIR MANAGER...
...BUT HE'TH EVEN WACKA THAN THE FAT BOY'TH.

CHARLIE STETTLER, THE **FAT BOYS'** MANAGER, HAS BEEN LOOKING FOR A CHANCE TO BOOST THE PROFILE OF HIS GROUP.

HMMM... THIS ALL SOUNDS NICE...

...BUT, THE FAT BOYS ARE PROBABLY GOING ON THE ROAD WITH **MICHAEL JACKSON.**

OH MY! IS THIS **TRUE,** CHAWLEE?

NOT AT ALL. I NEED YOU TO DRAFT A PRESS RELEASE RIGHT AWAY, ANYHOW.

CLICK

STETTLER'S RUSE IS MEANT TO MAKE THE FAT BOYS MORE ATTRACTIVE TO THEIR RECORD LABEL AND TO THE PROMOTER, WALKER, BUT HE ALSO ATTRACTS MAINSTREAM DAYTIME TELEVISION.

BUGGIN'!!

DON'T WORRY, BOYS. IF YOU GET NERVOUS AND DON'T KNOW WHAT TO DO ON CAMERA, THEN JUST GO...

"BRRRRRRRRRRRRRRR STICK 'EM... HUH-HA-HUH, STICK 'EM..."

MR. WALKER, I'VE DECIDED IT WOULD BE **BEST** TO HAVE THE **FAT BOYS** ON A RAP-CENTRIC TOUR RATHER THAN WITH **MICHAEL JACKSON.**

THAT'S COOL, BUT, I'M HAVING TROUBLE SECURING SPONSORSHIP.

OH YES, YOU MENTIONED THAT IN OUR LAST CALL. A FRIEND OF MINE BACK HOME IN **SWITZERLAND** HAS A WRIST-WATCH COMPANY CALLED **SWATCH.** HE'S LOOKING TO GAIN AWARENESS AND WILL INVEST **$350,000** TO SPONSOR OUR TOUR.

$350,000!

YEP, NOW GO TELL **RUSSELL SIMMONS** TO GO STICK THAT IN HIS FUCKIN' PIPE... HA HA HA!!

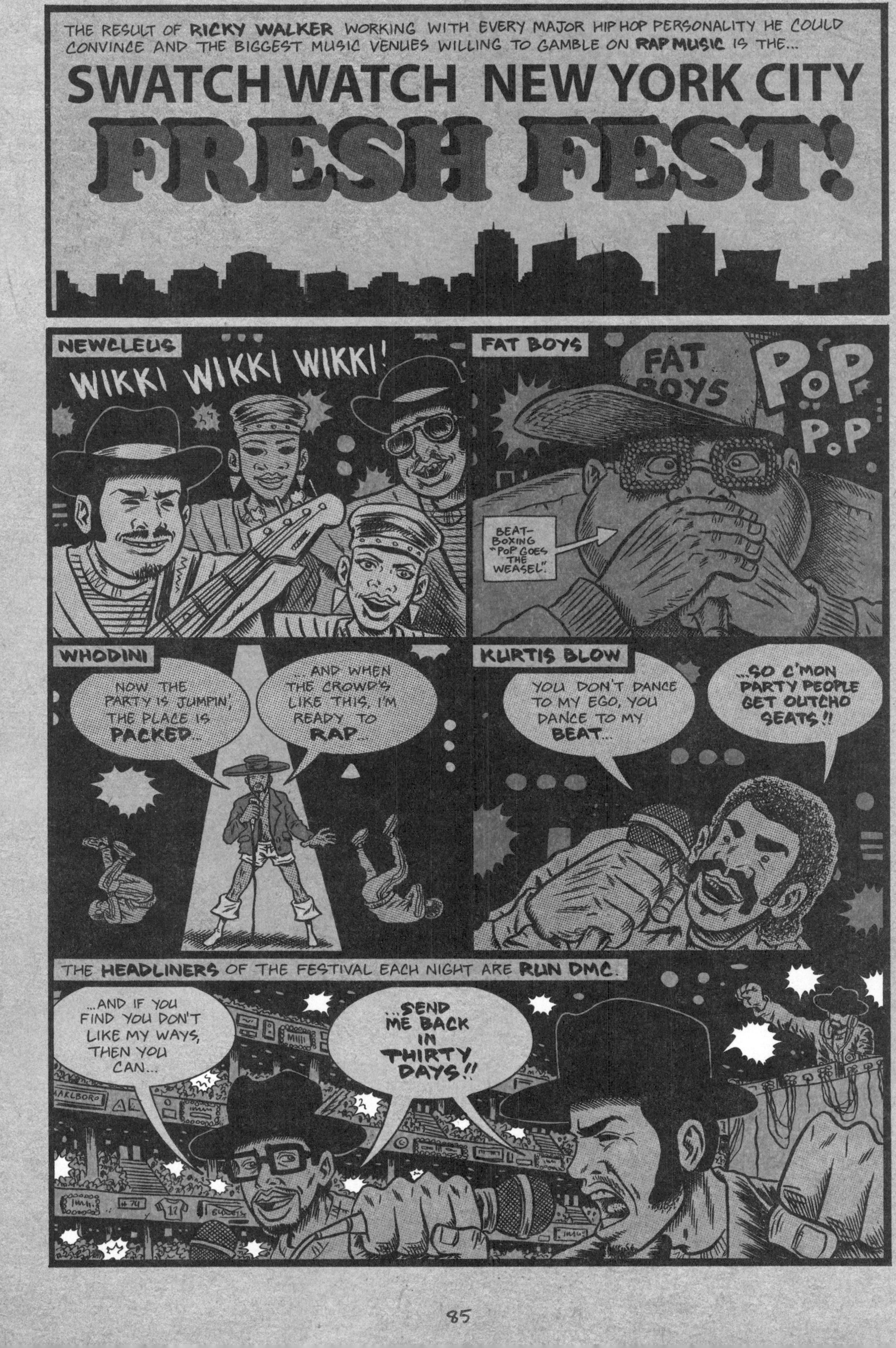
THE RESULT OF RICKY WALKER WORKING WITH EVERY MAJOR HIP HOP PERSONALITY HE COULD CONVINCE AND THE BIGGEST MUSIC VENUES WILLING TO GAMBLE ON RAP MUSIC IS THE...
SWATCH WATCH NEW YORK CITY
FRESH FEST!
NEWCLEUS
WIKKI WIKKI WIKKI!
FAT BOYS
FAT BOYS
POP POP P.O.P
BEAT-BOXING "POP GOES THE WEASEL".
WHODINI
NOW THE PARTY IS JUMPIN', THE PLACE IS PACKED...
...AND WHEN THE CROWD'S LIKE THIS, I'M READY TO RAP...
KURTIS BLOW
YOU DON'T DANCE TO MY EGO, YOU DANCE TO MY BEAT...
...SO C'MON PARTY PEOPLE GET OUTCHO SEATS!!
THE HEADLINERS OF THE FESTIVAL EACH NIGHT ARE RUN DMC.
...AND IF YOU FIND YOU DON'T LIKE MY WAYS, THEN YOU CAN...
...SEND ME BACK IN THIRTY DAYS!!

COVERING 27 **SOLD OUT** ARENAS IN MAJOR CITIES ACROSS THE COUNTRY, THE **FRESH FEST** IS NOT ONLY A FINANCIAL SUCCESS RAKING IN **$3.5 MILLION**, BUT IT'S ALSO SUCCESSFUL IN BRINGING **RAP MUSIC** TO A SEGMENT OF THE POPULATION THAT'S **NEVER** SEEN IT PERFORMED **LIVE**.

ALONG THE WAY, **CHARLIE STETTLER** MAKES SURE TO USE THE OPPORTUNITY TO INCREASE VISIBILITY TO THE **FAT BOYS** BEYOND THEIR NEW YORK CITY POPULARITY.

WHODINI'S **FREAKS COME OUT AT NIGHT** MUSIC VIDEO IS SHOT WHILE ON THE ROAD FOR **FRESH FEST**. **ANN CARLI**, THE MANAGER FOR CREATIVE SERVICES AT **JIVE RECORDS**, WANTED TO USE THAT MONEY TO MAKE A VIDEO FOR THE SONG SHE THOUGHT WAS STRONGER, BUT SHE WAS VETOED. SHE STILL FOUND A WAY TO GET IT IN THE VIDEO, THOUGH.

LOOK CLOSELY AT THE VIDEO. THE BOY YOU'LL SPY THROUGHOUT IS A YOUNG **JERMAINE DUPRI***. HIS FATHER DID SOME BEHIND THE SCENES WORK FOR THE TOUR.

* DUPRI HAS A LONG AND STORIED CAREER INCLUDING PRODUCING KRIS KROSS.

IT'S PROBABLY A STRONG BET THAT THE INDIVIDUAL WHO PROSPERED THE MOST FROM THE TOUR WAS **RUSSELL "RUSH" SIMMONS**.

...MADE AT LEETH'T A COUPLE DOLLAH'TH OFFA **ALL** THE AWTITH'T FROM THE FETH'T.

AS AN ARTIST, **HENRY CHALFANT** CHOOSES TO ISOLATE THE **GRAFFITI** ON THE TRAINS WHEN HE COMPOSES HIS **PHOTOGRAPHS**. THE GRAFF IS THE COMPLETE MESSAGE.

MARTHA COOPER IS JUST AS INTERESTED IN CAPTURING THE ENVIRONMENT AND THE ARTISTS THEMSELVES, WHEN SHE SHOOTS HER GRAFFITI FLICKS. THIS INSTINCT IS HEIGHTENED BY HER YEARS IN **PHOTOJOURNALISM**.

BOTH PHOTOGRAPHERS PURSUED THEIR OWN BOOK DEALS TO NO AVAIL.

I LIKE THE **GESTALT** OF OUR WORK TOGETHER.

I FEEL IT GIVES A MORE COMPLETE IDEA OF THIS MOVEMENT.

ART SPEAK...

THEIR PARTNERSHIP MAKES SENSE...

MARTY! A NEW **MIDG** BURNER!

SNAP!

87

EVEN WITH COMBINED EFFORT, NO NEW YORK PUBLISHERS WOULD TOUCH ANYTHING TO DO WITH GRAFFITI.

WHAT NEXT? YOU FUCKERS GONNA SHOW UP TO MY OFFICE TRYNA SELL ME A PICTURE BOOK FULL OF **3-CARD-MONTE** PLAYERS OR SUMP'IN?

THE DUO ENDS UP WITH **BRITISH** PUBLISHER **THAMES AND HUDSON** TO RELEASE THEIR BOOK, **SUBWAY ART**, IN 1984. THE **U.S.** EDITION IS TECHNICALLY A "**FOREIGN**" EDITION.

SUBWAY ART

Martha Cooper   **Henry Chalfant**

IN SPITE OF BEING POPULARLY REGARDED AS **THE MOST SHOPLIFTED BOOK IN THE WORLD**, **SUBWAY ART** HAS SOLD OVER **500,000** COPIES TO DATE.

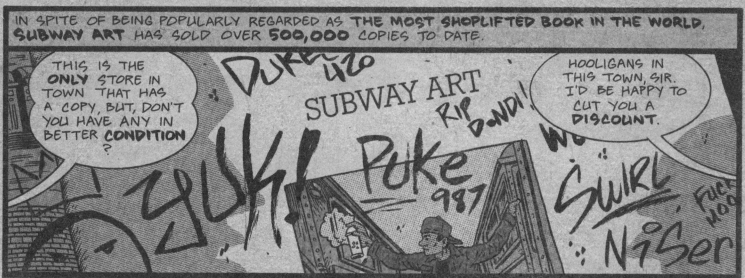

THIS IS THE **ONLY** STORE IN TOWN THAT HAS A COPY, BUT, DON'T YOU HAVE ANY IN BETTER **CONDITION**?

HOOLIGANS IN THIS TOWN, SIR. I'D BE HAPPY TO CUT YOU A **DISCOUNT**.

THE MUSICAL GROUP, **FULL FORCE** (3 BROTHERS, **BOW-LEGGED LOU**, **B-FINE**, AND **PAUL ANTHONY**, PLUS 3 COUSINS, **CURT-T-T**, **SHY-SHY**, AND **BABY GERRY**) HELPED WRITE AND PRODUCE SEVERAL OF **KURTIS BLOW'S** 1984 PROJECTS INCLUDING THE HIT SINGLE, **BASKETBALL**.

THE GROUP KEPT GETTING REJECTED FOR RECORD DEALS WHEN THEY DECIDED THAT PRODUCING COULD BE THEIR FOOTHOLD INTO THE INDUSTRY. **FULL FORCE** HAPPEN TO BE NEIGHBORS WITH SOME OF **WHODINI'S** BACK-UP DANCERS WHO JUST GOT BACK FROM **FRESH FEST**.

IN THE HANDS OF **FULL FORCE**, THOSE BACK-UP B-BOYS BECOME **UTFO** (**KANGOL KID**, **DOCTOR ICE**, **EDUCATED RAPPER** AND **MIX MASTER ICE**). FULL FORCE PRODUCES THEIR 12-INCH DEBUT, **HANGING OUT**, AND IT FINDS A HOME AT THE LABEL **SELECT RECORDS**.

...WE'RE ACCUSTOMED TO THE QUESTION...

...UNTOUCHABLE FORCE ORGANIZATION.

AS IS CUSTOM, **SELECT RECORDS** SENDS **HANGING OUT** TO CLUB AND RADIO DJS FOR PROMOTION. THIS INCLUDES **KOOL DJ RED ALERT**.

THIS RECORD ISN'T BAD, BUT THE **B-SIDE** IS THE BANGER.

FULL FORCE, UTFO, AND THE EXECS AT SELECT RECORDS ALL LET **RED ALERT** KNOW HIS MISTAKE.

HA HA HA... JUS' TRUS' ME, Y'ALL...

THE **B-SIDE** TRACK WAS SLAPPED TOGETHER WHEN **FULL FORCE** TOLD **UTFO** TO COME UP WITH A SERIES OF RHYMES ABOUT THEIR PURSUIT OF A GIRL WHO REJECTS THEM ALL. THEY COME UP WITH...

ROXANNE, ROXANNE, CAN'T YOU UNDERSTAND?

RED ALERT BREAKS THE HIT WHICH QUICKLY SELLS AROUND **500,000** UNITS.

ROXANNE, ROXANNE, I WANNA BE YOUR MAN...

THIS LAUNCHES **UTFO** INTO STARDOM. SOMEHOW, WHILE PREPARING FOR A BIG **NYC** PERFORMANCE, THE GROUP DOESN'T SHOW UP FOR A SCHEDULED BOOKING ON **MR. MAGIC'S RAP ATTACK** RADIO SHOW TO PROMOTE THE EVENT.

THEY THINK THEY C'N JUST STAND-UP **SIR JUICE**?

MARLEY!? GIT OVER HERE. WE HAVE TO **SERVE** THEY ASSES...

AIR

QUEENSBRIDGE HOUSING PROJECTS...

HEY, SHANTE! YO, YOUNG'UN, I HEARD YOU GOT RHYMES?

MARLEY MARL?

WELL, WHY YOU ASKING, SUCKA?

GOO...

IF YOU'RE AS NICE ON THE MIC AS I HEAR, I'LL HOOK YOU UP WIT' SOME SERGIO VALENTES.

DUNG-AREES?

MR. MAGIC, MARLEY MARL, AND THEIR MANAGER FLY TY CONSPIRE TO MAKE A SONG THAT THEY CAN PLAY ON THEIR RADIO SHOW TO DISS UTFO. THIS IS WHERE 14-YEAR-OLD LOLITA SHANTE GOODEN COMES IN. YOU MAY KNOW HER BY HER MONIKER...

...MY NAME IS ROXANNE...

MR. MAGIC

...AND THEY CALL ME SHANTE.

MARLEY MARL HAS BEEN AMASSING RECORD-ING EQUIPMENT WITH EVERY SPARE DIME HE CAN MUSTER. HE'S BEEN AT IT FOR A FEW YEARS AT THIS POINT.

...HE SAID "YEAH YOUR MOTHER'S NAME IS MARY"...

...BUT, ALL HE WANTS TO DO IS JUST BUST A CHERRY...

USING THE ROXANNE, ROXANNE INSTRU-MENTAL, MARLEY MARL AND THE NEWLY CHRISTENED ROXANNE SHANTE GO RIGHT FOR UTFO'S JUGULAR OVER THE AIRWAVES IN NEW YORK CITY AND PHILADELPHIA.

ROXANNE FEEL IT!!

A WORLD PREMIERE !!

?

YOU SEE, **MR. MAGIC** SIMULCASTS IN BOTH MAJOR MARKETS DURING **1984**. THIS IS HOW **L.G. GOODMAN** OF **POP ART RECORDS** IN PHILADELPHIA HEARS **SHANTE** AND SMELLS AN OPPORTUNITY.

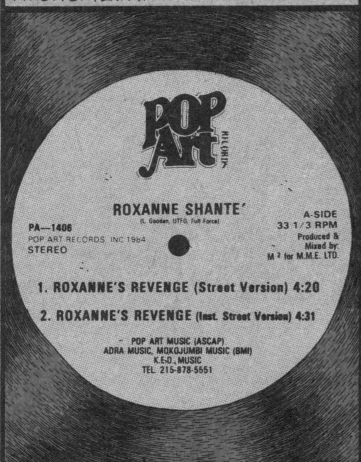

THE FIRST **5,000** COPIES OF **ROXANNE'S REVENGE** WERE LITERALLY RECORDED STRAIGHT FROM **MR. MAGIC'S** RADIO SHOW BEFORE BOOKING STUDIO-TIME TO MAKE A BETTER PRODUCED VERSION. **250,000** COPIES LATER **ROXANNE SHANTE** LEAVES HIGH SCHOOL BEHIND.

UTFO AND THEIR PRODUCERS **FULL FORCE** RUSH TO RECORD A RESPONSE TRACK WITH THEIR OWN FEMALE MC DUBBED **THE REAL ROXANNE.**

ROXANNE SHANTE NEVER GOT THOSE **SERGIO VALENTE** JEANS THAT **MARLEY** PROMISED HER, IF YOU'RE WONDERING. AS A CONSOLATION SHE JUST BECOMES ONE OF THE GREATEST **BATTLE MCS** IN HIP HOP AND WHETHER SHE KNOWS IT OR NOT, THE **WAR** IS JUST BEGINNING...

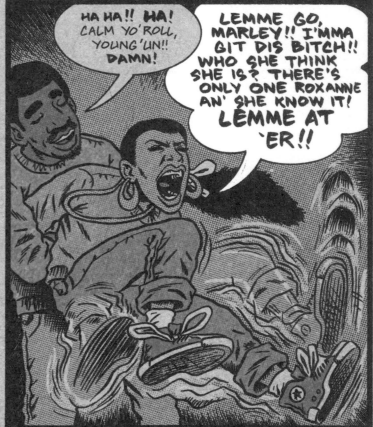

WHEN **KRS-ONE** FINISHES HIS **2 MONTH** BID IN THE **BRONX HOUSE OF DETENTION**, HE ENDS UP STAYING AT THE **FRANKLIN ARMORY MENS SHELTER** ALONGSIDE AT LEAST **650** OTHER HOMELESS SOULS AT ANY GIVEN TIME.

YOU BEEN LOOKIN' FOR ME, MAN?

YO, KRS!

THEY SAY YOU'ZA SPIRITUAL, DUDE, NO?

YO MOMMA'S TITTY NIPPLE!!

EVEN THOUGH I **KILLED** A MAN ONCE, I'M WORKING HARD TO FIND AND FOLLOW **JESUS**, OUR SAVIOR.

UH... HUH, YEAH. IT'S WRONG TO TAKE A LIFE BUT SOMETIMES YOU MUST PROTEC' YO'SELF...

YEAH, **MUH FUGGA** GOT ON MY LAST NERVE.

...CRIED LIKE A LITTLE **BITCH-DOG** AT THE END, TOO...

HA HA... YOU HAVE A GOOD DAY, LI'L-BAT.

AFTER A FEW MONTHS IN THE SHELTER, **KRS** NOTICES A NEW SOCIAL WORKER NAMED **SCOTT STERLING** WHO LOOKS LIKE AN EASY ENOUGH MARK.

TOSS ME LIKE FIVE **TRAIN TOKENS**, BRUH. I'M HUNTING FOR SOME **EMPLOYMENT** LEADS I'M FOLLOWING UP ON.

NO...

HUH?

"...I HEARD YOUR **LAZY** BEHIND HAS BEEN SELLING YOUR DAILY ALLOTMENT OF TOKENS FOR HEAVEN KNOWS WHAT."

LET'S GO GET SOME **CHINESE**.

LITTLE DOES **KRS-ONE**, OR ANY OTHER MEN IN THE SHELTER SYSTEM, KNOW THAT **SCOTT STERLING** HAPPENS TO MOONLIGHT EVERY EVENING AS THE **HOUSE DJ** AT THE **BROADWAY INTERNATIONAL** HIP HOP NIGHTCLUB.

NEXT

KRS-ONE AND SCOTT LA ROCK TEAM UP? BELIEVE IT!!

“This good shit ain't done yet.”

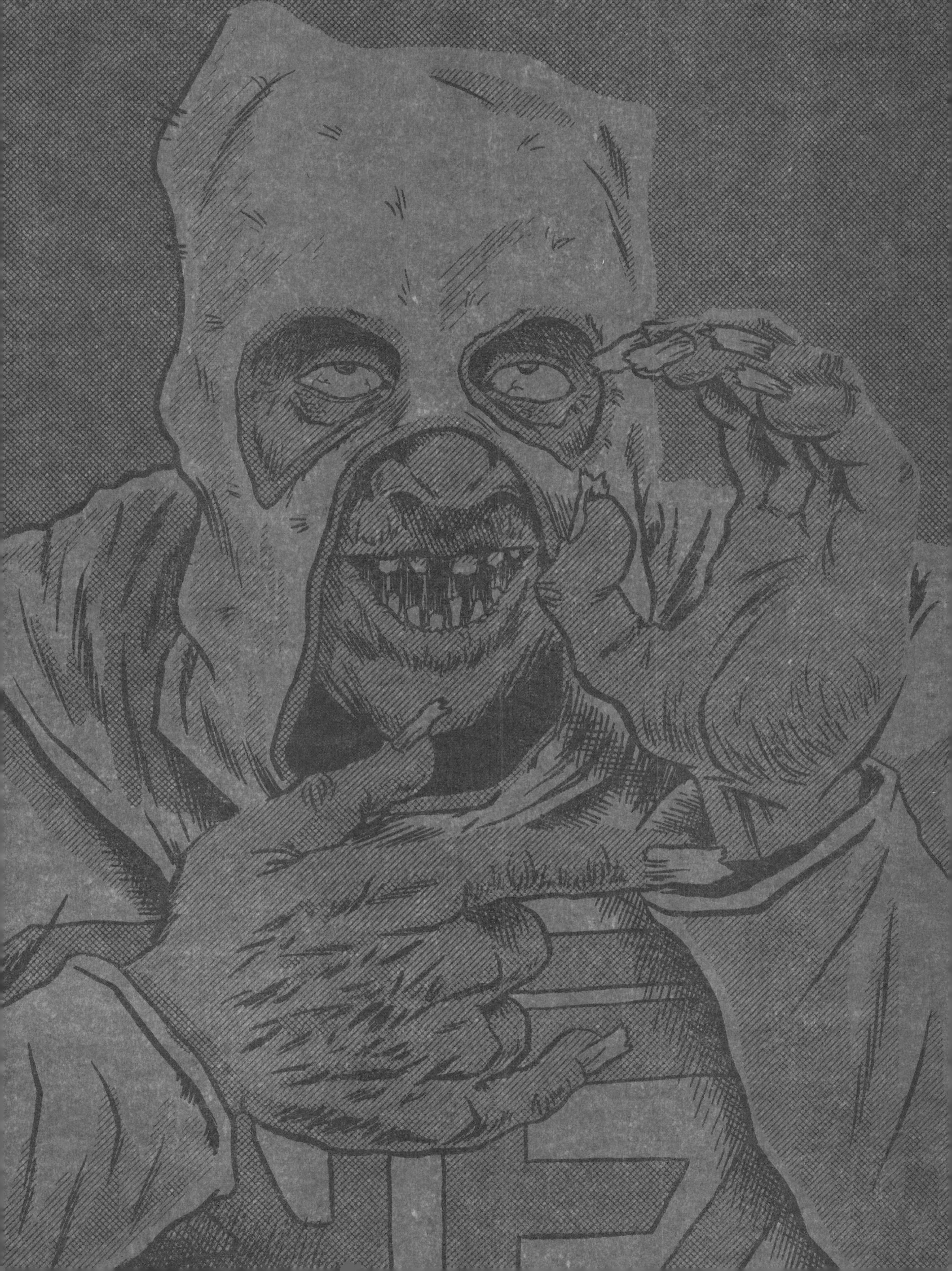

PINUPS

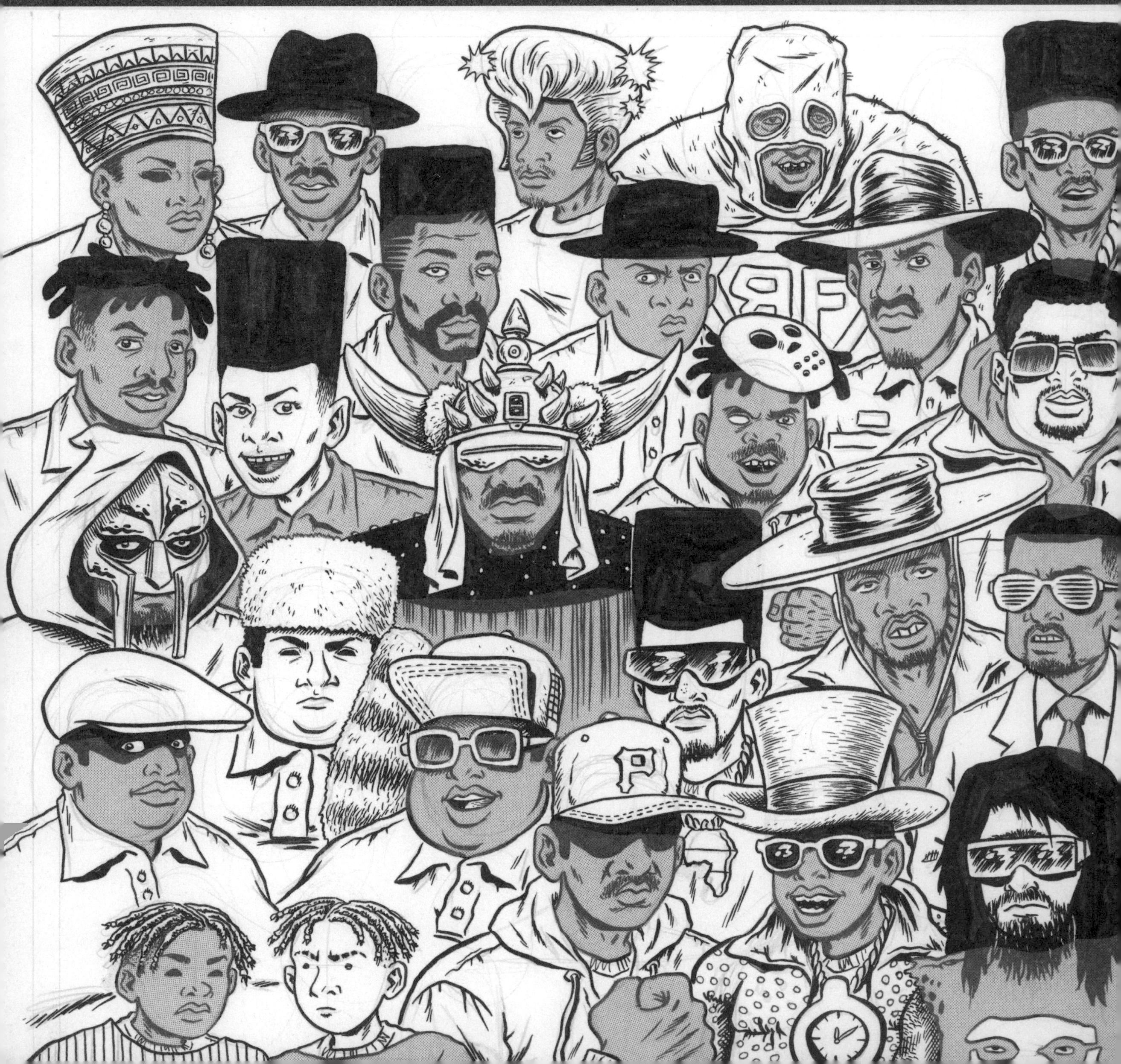

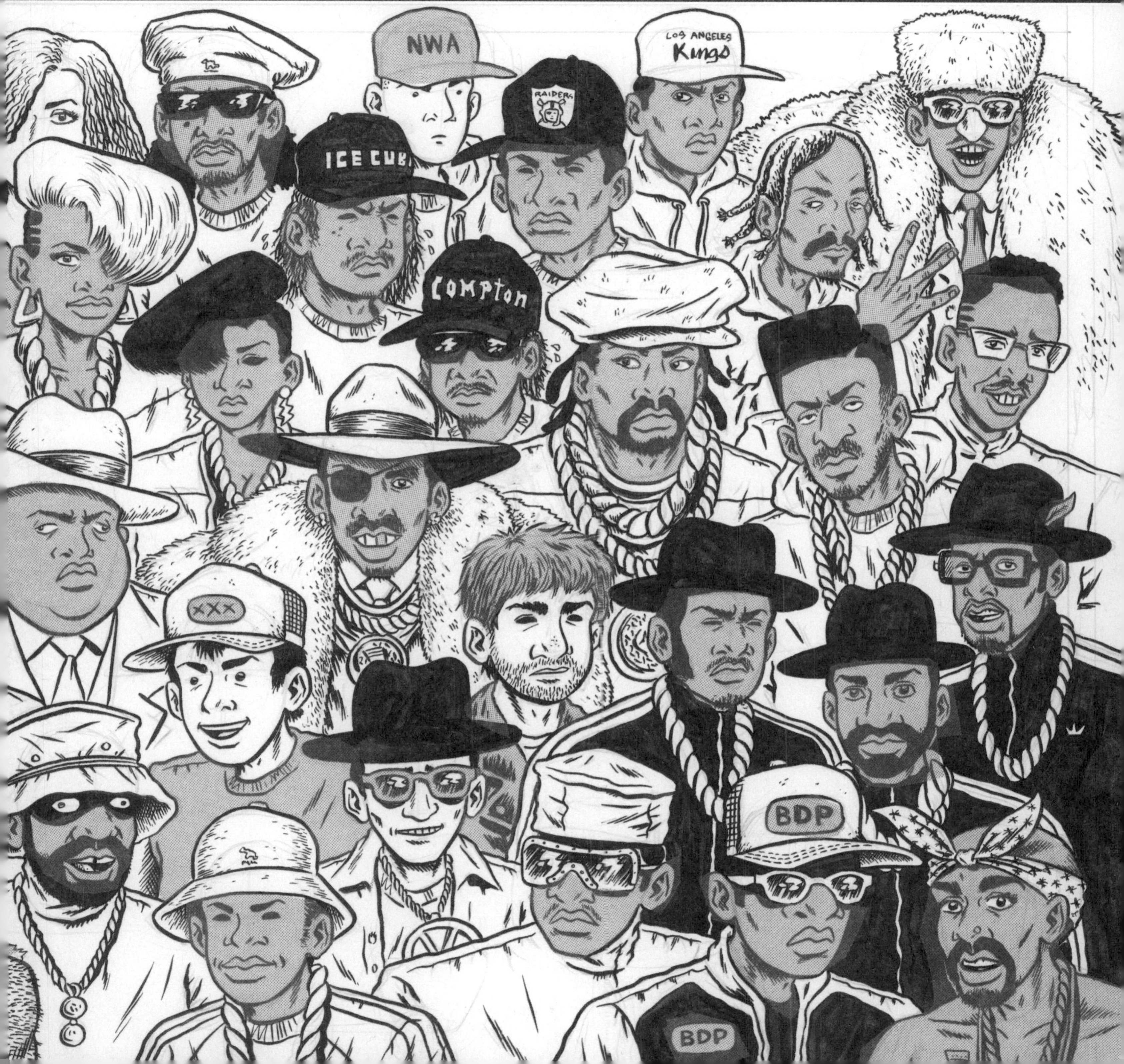
NWA
LOS ANGELES
Kings
RAIDERS
ICE CUB
Compton
XXX
BDP
BDP

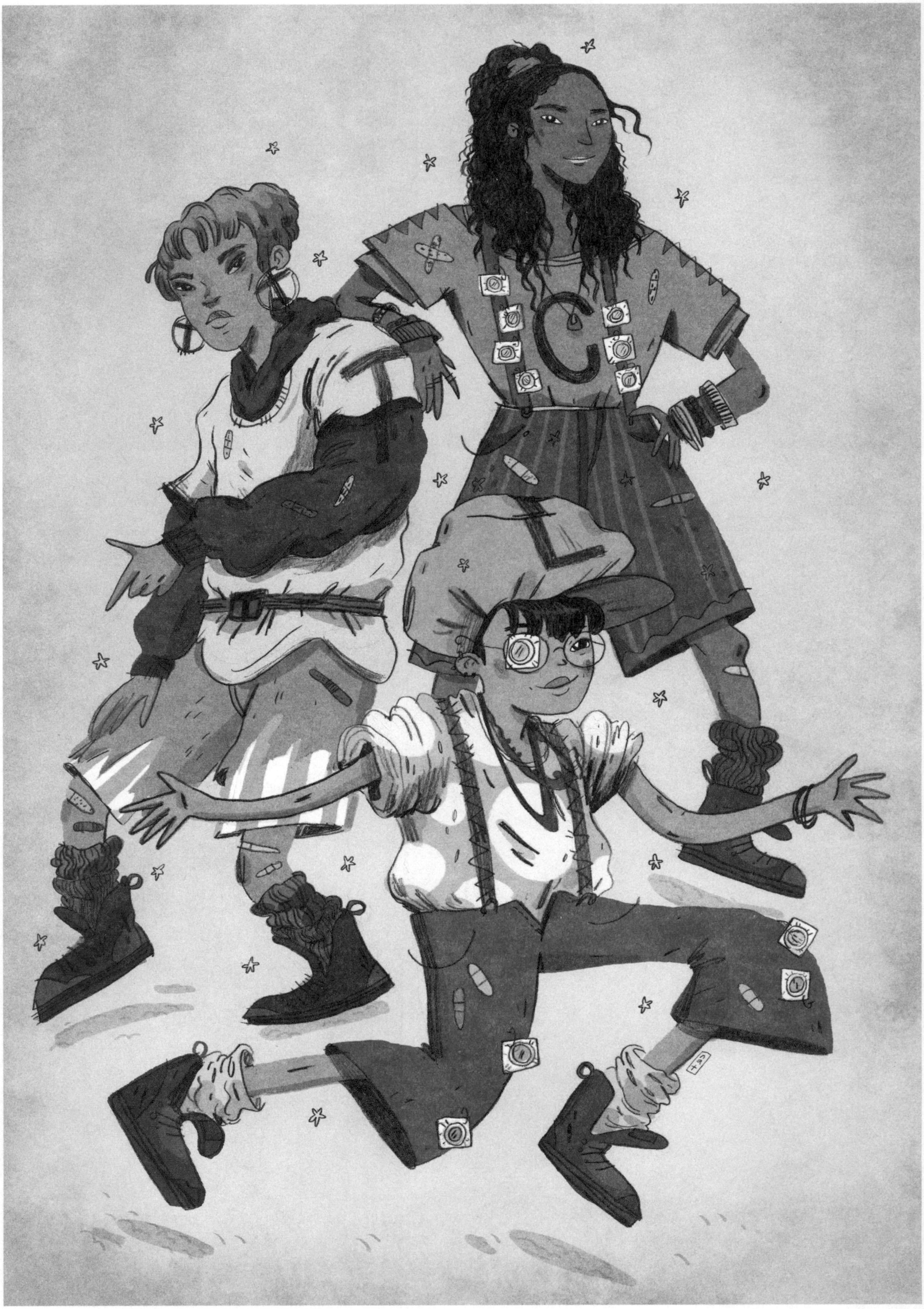

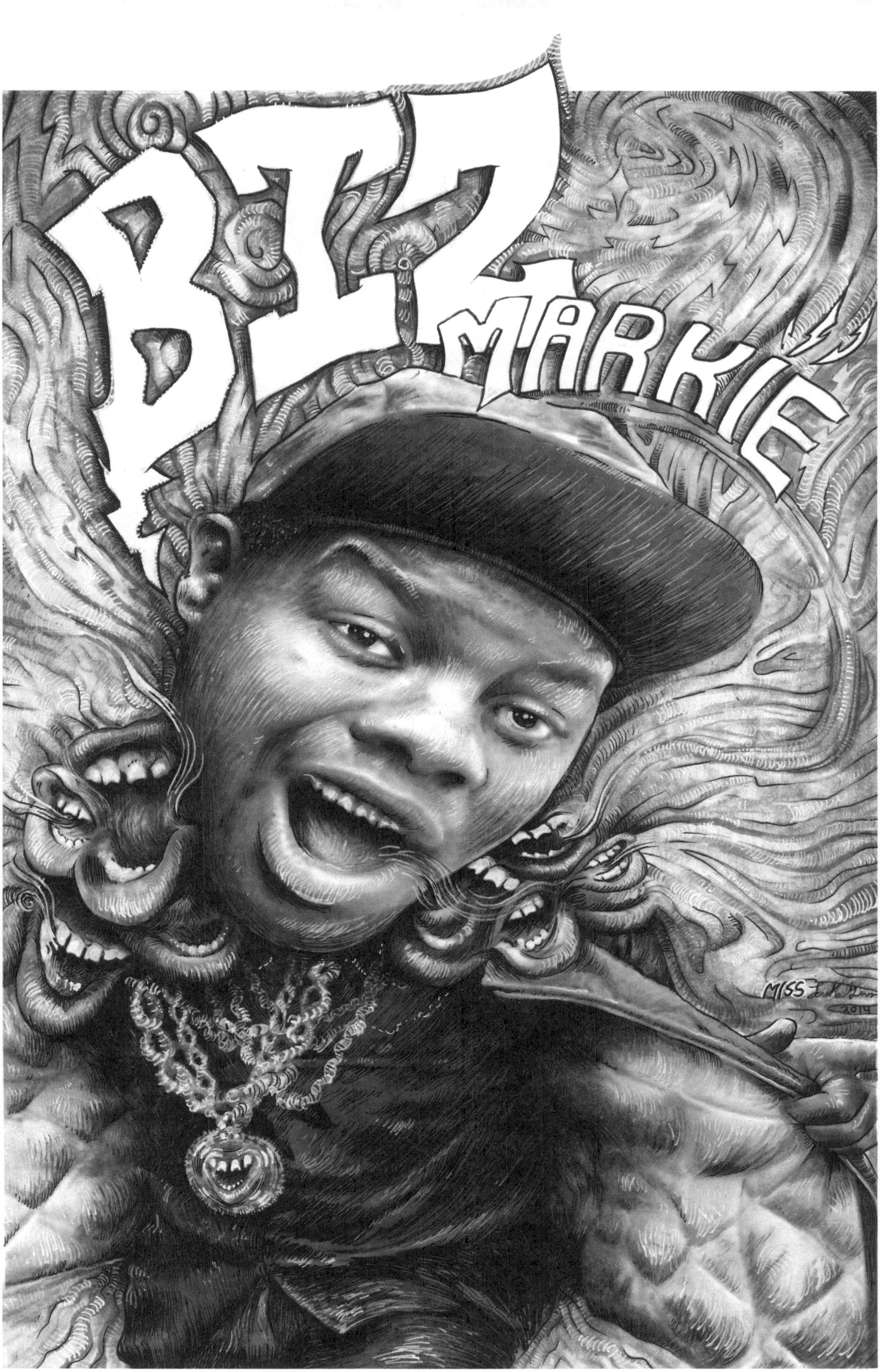
BIZ
MARKIE

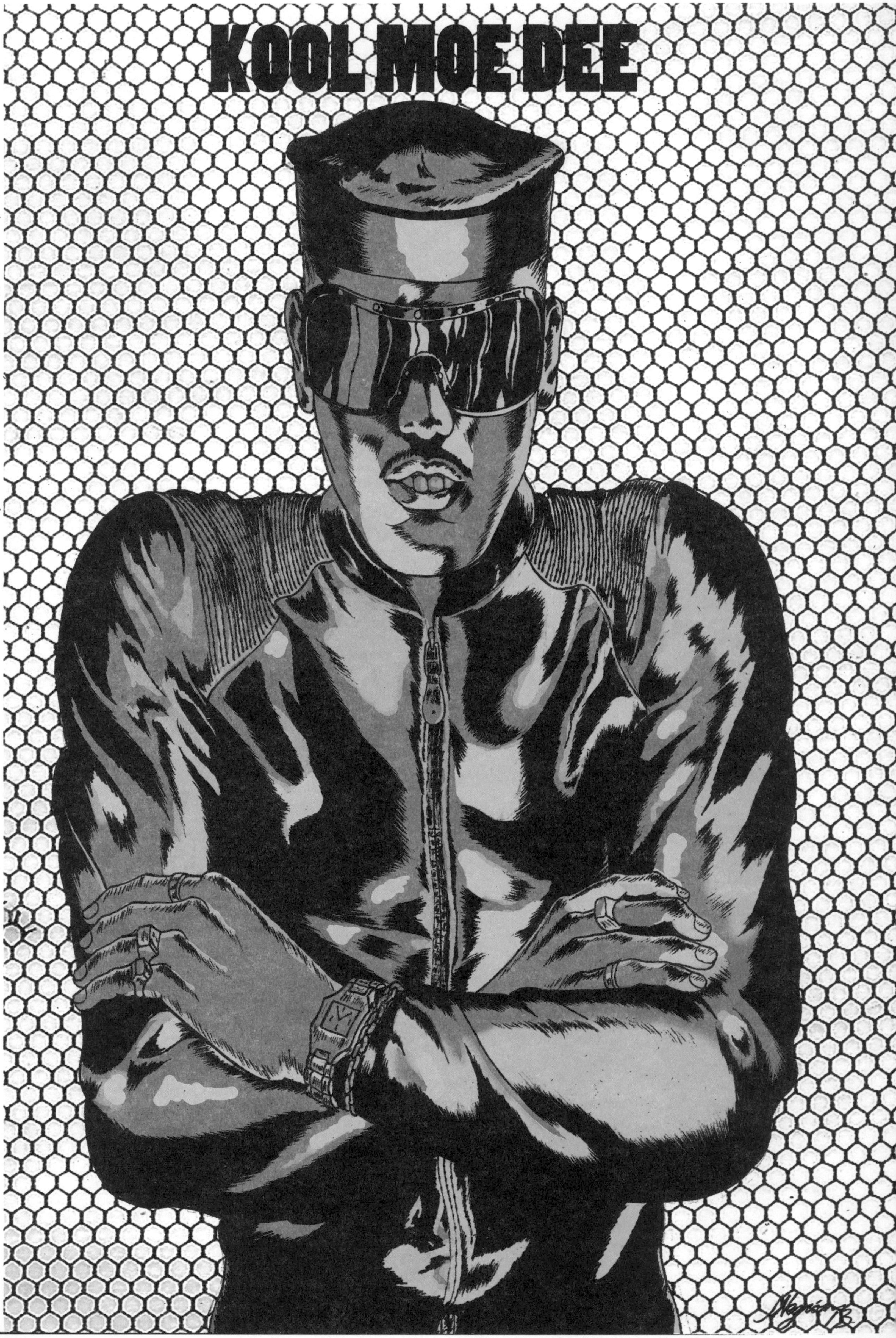
KOOL MOE DEE

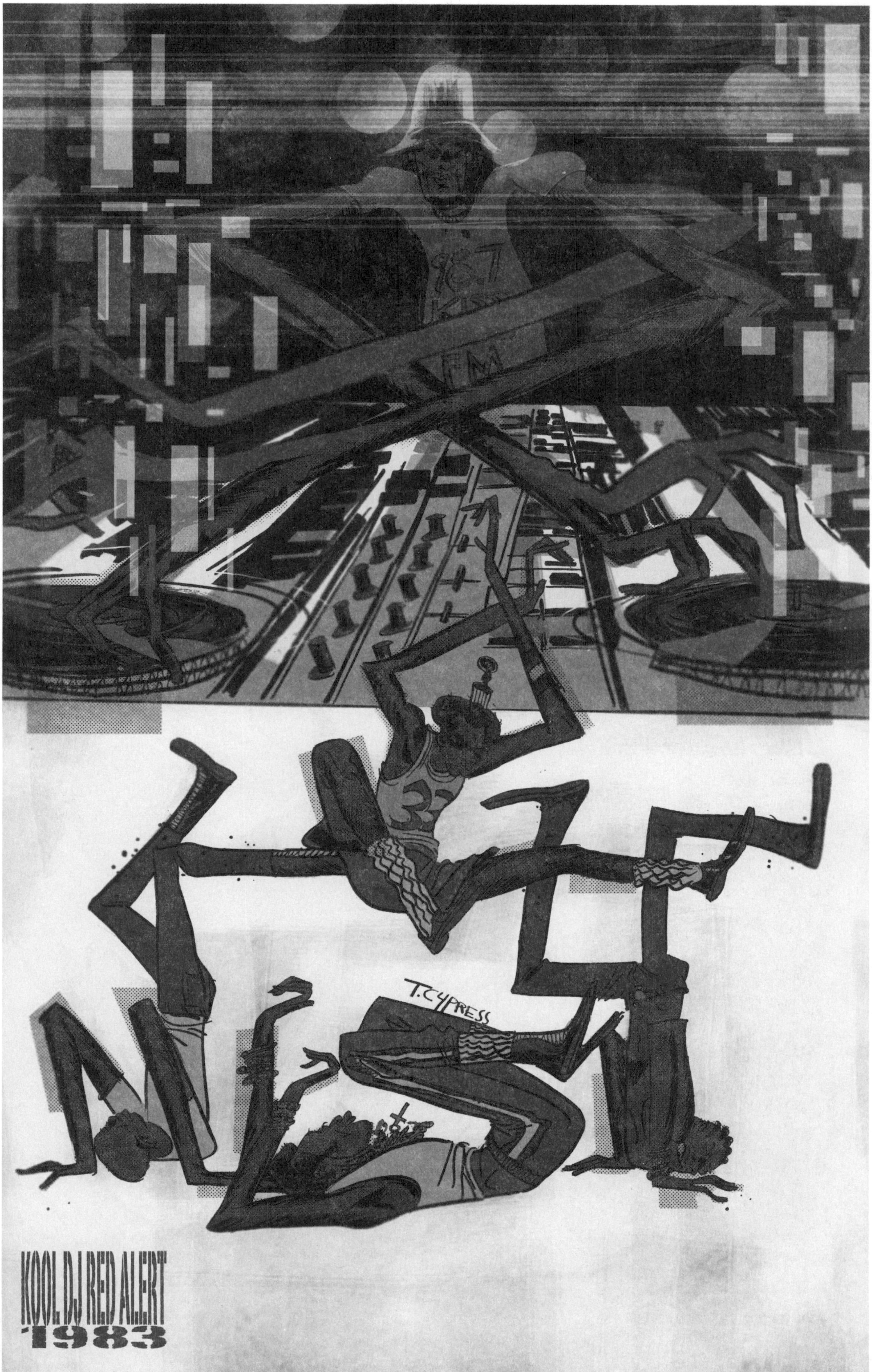
98.7
KISS
FM
33
T.CYPRESS
KOOL DJ RED ALERT
1983

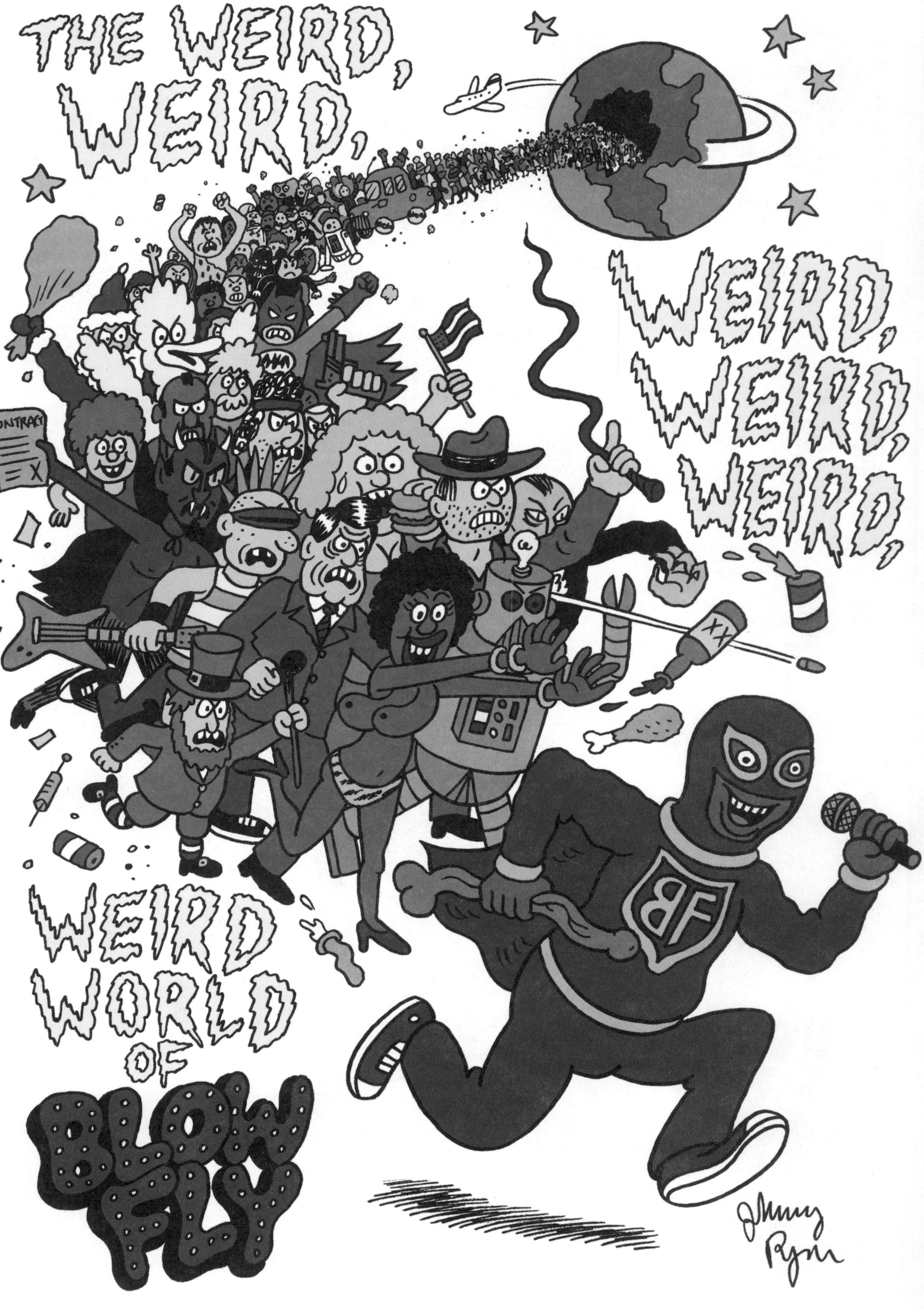
THE WEIRD, WEIRD,
WEIRD, WEIRD, WEIRD,
WEIRD WORLD OF
BLOWFLY
CONTRACT
BF

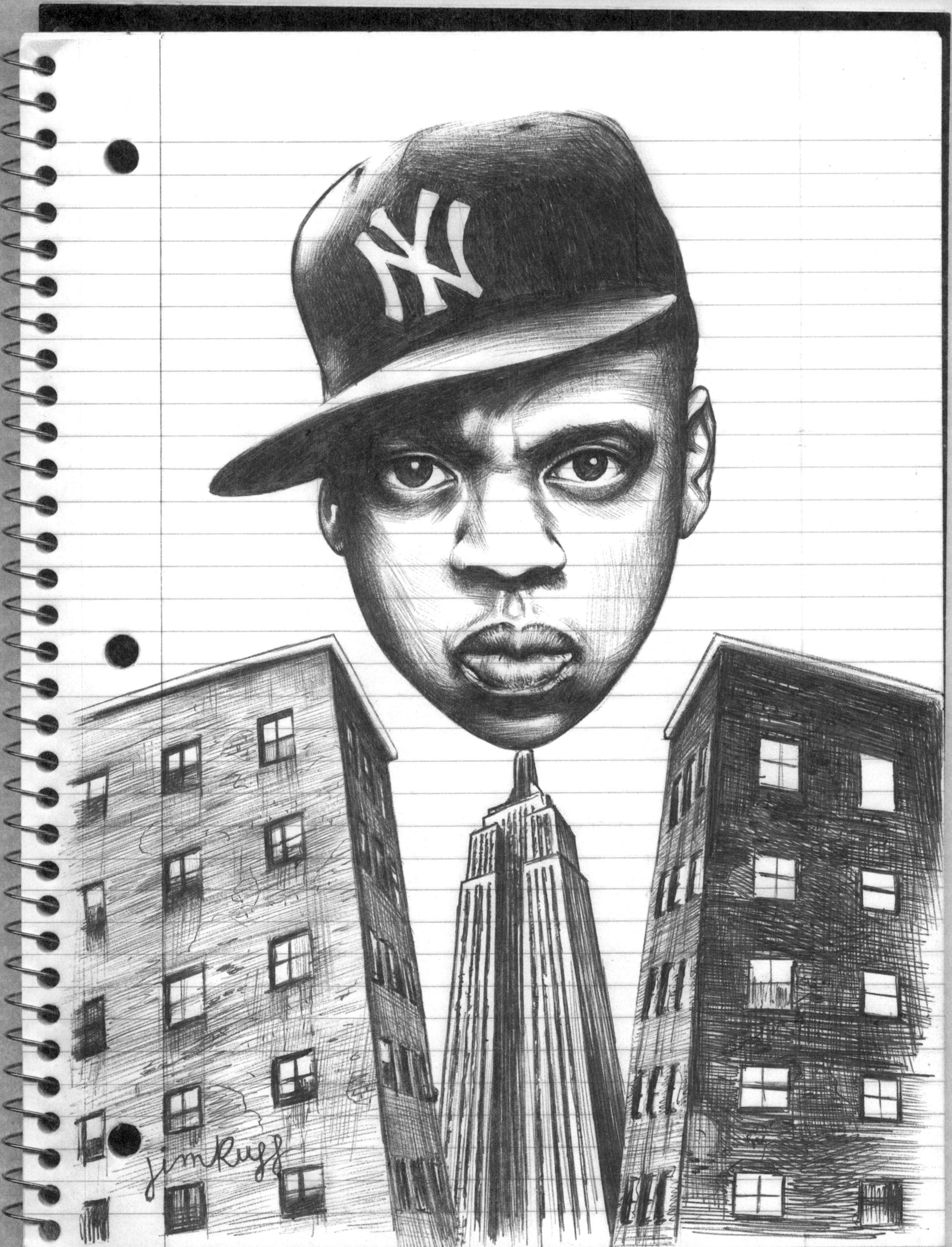
NY
jimRugg

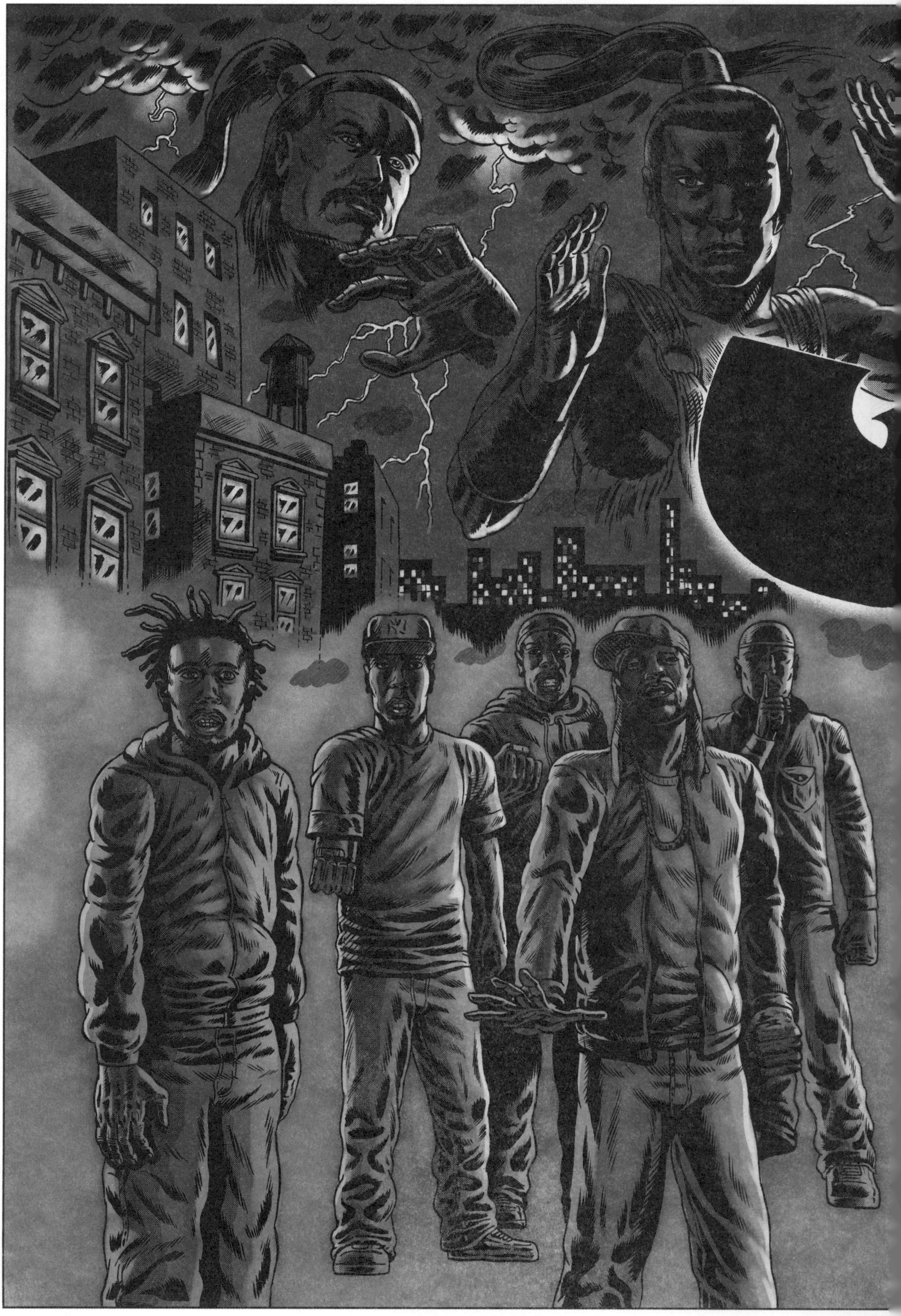

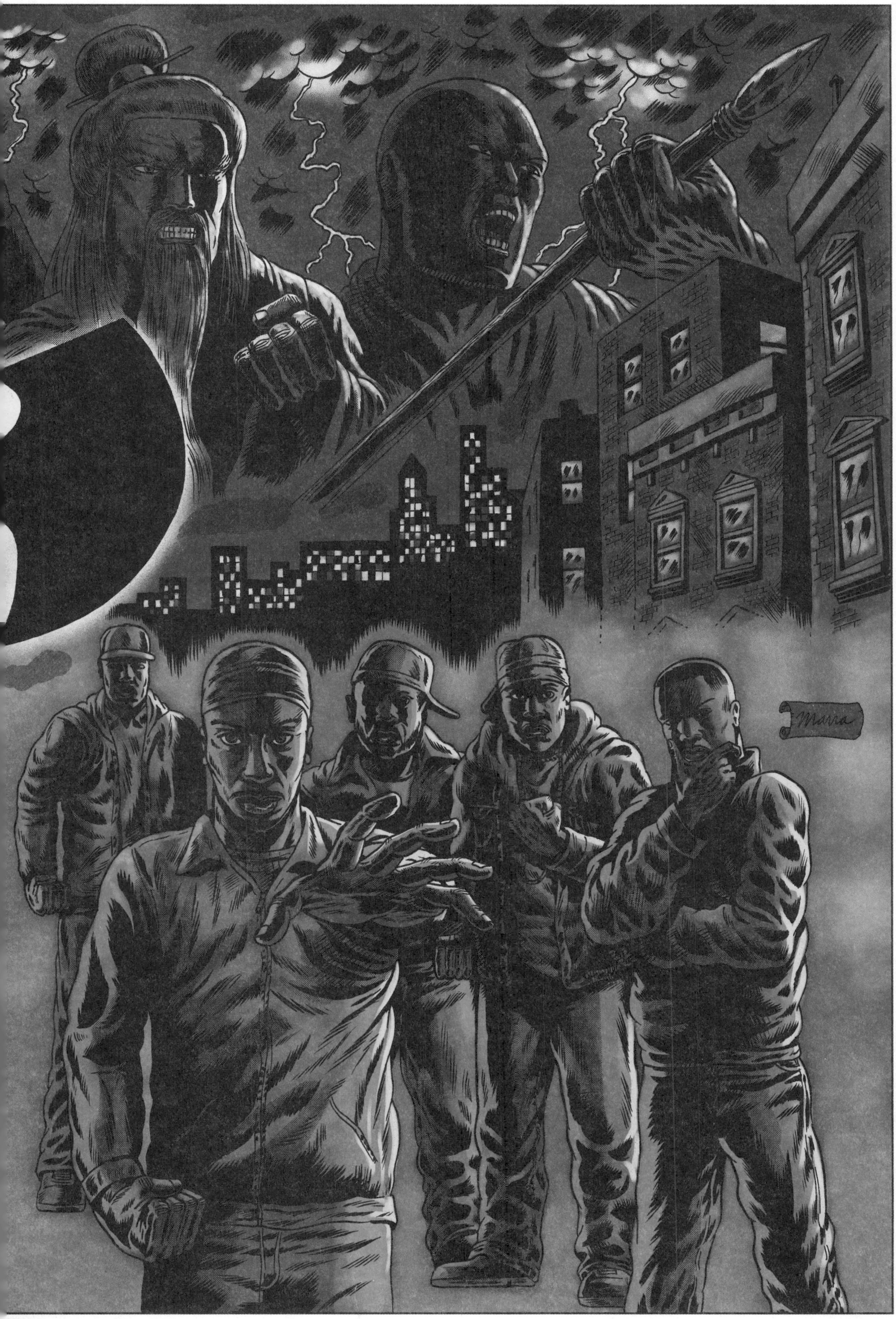
Marra

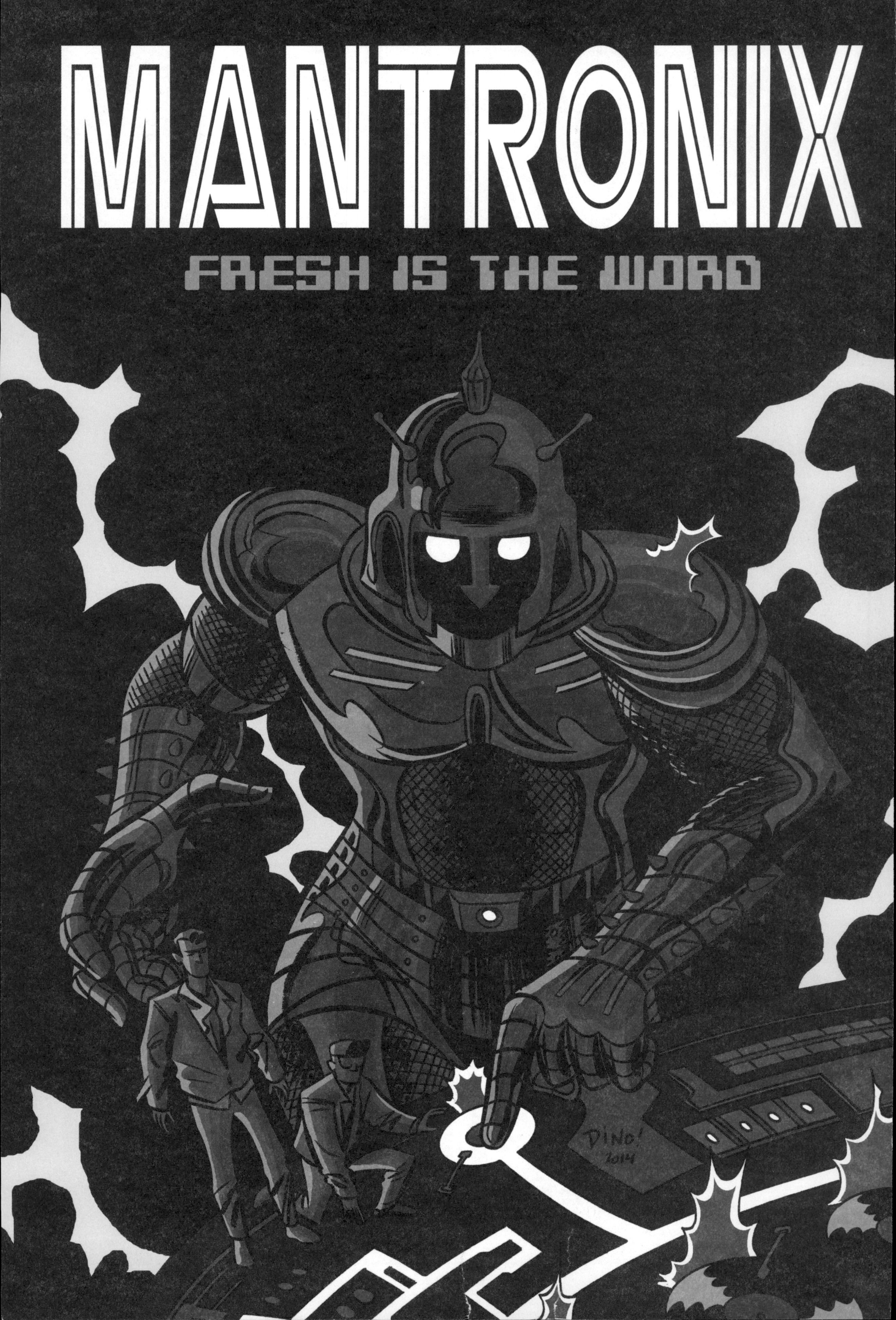
MANTRONIX
FRESH IS THE WORD
DINO!
2014

ANDRE ROMELLE YOUNG YEARS ACTIVE: 1984 – PRESENT

STILL
D.R.E.

<u>JACK KIRBY</u> (SUPER-HERO COMIC ARTIST):

"...IN OTHER WORDS, MY AMBITION WAS ALWAYS TO BE A PERFECT PICTURE OF AN AMERICAN. AN AMERICAN IS A GUY, A RICH GUY WITH A FAMILY, A DECENT GUY WITH A FAMILY, WITH AS MANY KIDS AS HE LIKES, DOING WHAT HE WANTS, WORKING WITH PEOPLE THAT HE LIKES, AND ENJOYING HIMSELF TO HIS VERY OLD AGE."

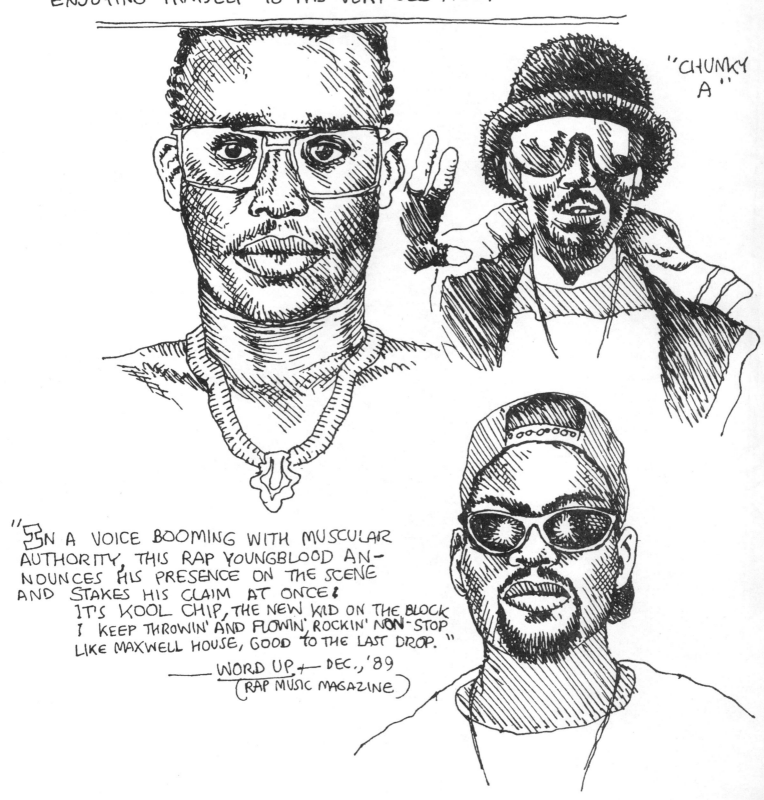

"CHUNKY A"

"IN A VOICE BOOMING WITH MUSCULAR AUTHORITY, THIS RAP YOUNGBLOOD ANNOUNCES HIS PRESENCE ON THE SCENE AND STAKES HIS CLAIM AT ONCE:
IT'S KOOL CHIP, THE NEW KID ON THE BLOCK
I KEEP THROWIN' AND FLOWIN', ROCKIN' NON-STOP
LIKE MAXWELL HOUSE, GOOD TO THE LAST DROP."
— WORD UP + DEC., '89
(RAP MUSIC MAGAZINE)

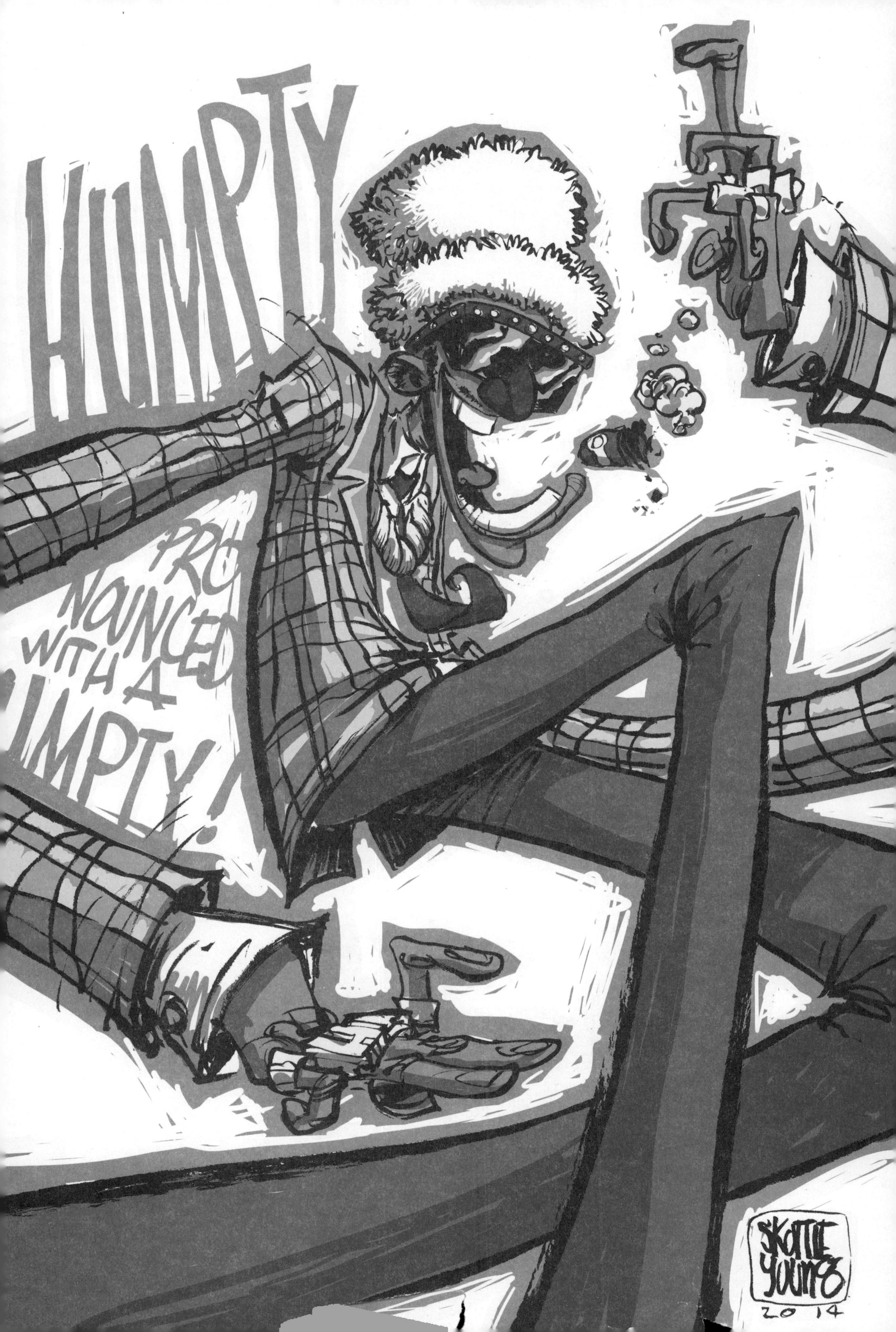
HUMPTY
PRO
NOUNCED
WITH A
MPTY!
SKOTTIE YOUNG
2014

BIBLIOGRAPHY

ADLER, BILL. **TOUGHER THAN LEATHER: THE AUTHORIZED BIOGRAPHY OF RUN-DMC**. NEW YORK: NEW AMERICAN LIBRARY, 1987. PRINT.

CHANG, JEFF. **CAN'T STOP, WON'T STOP: A HISTORY OF THE HIP-HOP GENERATION**. NEW YORK: ST. MARTIN'S, 2005. PRINT.

CHARNAS, DAN. **THE BIG PAYBACK: THE HISTORY OF THE BUSINESS OF HIP-HOP**. NEW YORK, NY: NEW AMERICAN LIBRARY, 2010. PRINT.

FRESH, FREDDY. **FREDDY FRESH PRESENTS THE RAP RECORDS**. SAINT PAUL, MN: NERBY PUB. LLC, 2004. PRINT.

FRICKE, JIM AND CHARLIE AHEARN. **YES YES Y'ALL: THE EXPERIENCE MUSIC PROJECT ORAL HISTORY OF HIP-HOP'S FIRST DECADE**. CAMBRIDGE, MA: DA CAPO, 2002. PRINT.

ICE-T, AND DOUGLAS CENTURY. **ICE: A MEMOIR OF GANGSTER LIFE AND REDEMPTION-- FROM SOUTH CENTRAL TO HOLLYWOOD**. NEW YORK: ONE WORLD/BALLANTINE, 2011. PRINT.

JENKINS, SACHA. **EGO TRIP'S BOOK OF RAP LISTS**. NEW YORK: ST. MARTIN'S GRIFFIN, 1999. PRINT.

SIMMONS, RUSSELL, AND NELSON GEORGE. **LIFE AND DEF: SEX, DRUGS, MONEY, AND GOD**. NEW YORK, NY: CROWN, 2001. PRINT.

WHISLER, LEAH. **DEF JAM RECORDINGS: THE FIRST 25 YEARS OF THE LAST GREAT RECORD LABEL**. NEW YORK: RIZZOLI, 2011. PRINT.

REFERENCE

FILM/DOCUMENTARIES

1. **WILD STYLE**, CHARLIE AHEARN
2. **STYLE WARS**, TONY SILVER & HENRY CHALFANT
3. **BEAT THIS!: A HIP HOP HISTORY**, DICK FONTAINE
4. **RHYME AND REASON**, PETER SPIRER
5. **BEEF** (SERIES), PETER SPIRER
6. **AND YOU DON'T STOP: 30 YEARS OF HIP HOP**, RICHARD LOWE, DANA HEINZ PERRY
7. **NY77: THE COOLEST YEAR IN HELL**, HENRY CORRA
8. **SOMETHING FROM NOTHING: THE ART OF RAP**, ICE T, ANDY BAYBUTT
9. **UPRISING: HIP HOP AND THE L.A. RIOTS**, MARK FORD
10. **RAP: LOOKING FOR THE PERFECT BEAT**
11. **PLANET ROCK: THE STORY OF HIP-HOP AND THE CRACK GENERATION**, RICHARD LOWE, MARTIN TORGOFF
12. **THE SHOW**, BRIAN ROBBINS
13. **SCRATCH**, DOUG PRAY

MORE VIDEO

1. **RED BULL MUSIC ACADEMY LECTURE SERIES** (INTERNET SERIES)
2. **UNSUNG** (TV SERIES)
3. **BEHIND THE MUSIC** (TV SERIES)
4. **BIOGRAPHY** (TV SERIES)

WEBSITES/PODCASTS

1. THAFOUNDATION.COM (INTERVIEWS BY JAY QUAN & TROY L. SMITH)
2. DISCOGS.COM
3. WHOSAMPLED.COM
4. OLDSCHOOLHIPHOP.COM
5. THECOMBATJACKSHOW.COM (INTERVIEW PODCAST SERIES)

SOUNDTRACK SELECTION

1. **HARD TIMES**, RUN DMC (PROFILE)
2. **PARTY TIME**, KURTIS BLOW (MERCURY)
3. **GETTIN' MONEY**, DR. JECKYLL & MR. HYDE (PROFILE)
4. **MONEY (DOLLAR BILL Y'ALL**, JIMMY SPICER (SPRING)
5. **YOU'VE GOTTA BELIEVE**, LOVEBUG STARSKI (FEVER)
6. **PROBLEMS OF THE WORLD TODAY**, FEARLESS FOUR (ELEKTRA)
7. **GAMES PEOPLE PLAY**, SWEET GEE (FEVER)
8. **2,3, BREAK**, THE B-BOYS (VINTERTAINMENT)
9. **PUNK ROCK RAP**, THE COLD CRUSH BROTHERS, (TUFF CITY)
10. **REALITY**, DISCO THREE (SUTRA)
11. **THE HAUNTED HOUSE OF ROCK**, WHODINI (JIVE)
12. **JAM ON REVENGE**, NEWCLEUS (MAYHEW)
13. **CHECK OUT THE RADIO**, SPECTRUM CITY (VANGUARD)
14. **IT'S YOURS**, T LA ROCK (PARTYTIME)
15. **JUST HAVIN' FUN**, DOUG E. FRESH (ENJOY)
16. **THE ORIGINAL HUMAN BEAT BOX**, DOUG E. FRESH (VINTERTAINMENT)
17. **ROCK BOX**, RUN DMC (PROFILE)
18. **STEP OFF**, GRANDMASTER MELLE MEL (SUGAR HILL)
19. **ESCAPE** (ALBUM), WHODINI (JIVE)
20. **RUN-DMC** (ALBUM), RUN DMC (PROFILE)
21. **BASKETBALL**, KURTIS BLOW (MERCURY)
22. **EGO TRIP** (ALBUM), KURTIS BLOW (MERCURY)
23. **I NEED A BEAT**, LL COOL J (DEF JAM)
24. **ROXANNE, ROXANNE**, UTFO (SELECT)
25. **ROXANNE'S REVENGE**, ROXANNE SHANTE (POP ART)

Funky Index

ED PISKOR, HOMESTEAD, PA (1982 ~ _____)
                                    FILL IN THE BLANK

HIP HOP FAMILY TREE HAS BROUGHT ED
ALL OVER THE UNITED STATES AND THE
WORLD. IN FACT, AT THIS VERY MOMENT
HE'S WRITING THIS SELF-AGGRANDIZING
PSEUDO-BIOGRAPHY IN DENMARK WHERE HE'S
TEACHING A TWO-WEEK WORKSHOP TO THE
NEXT GENERATION OF CARTOONISTS.

THIS SERIES HAS BEEN TRANSLATED INTO
5 LANGUAGES SO FAR AND PISKOR'S
SOLD THE RIGHTS FOR THERE TO BE A FILM
OR TV SHOW WHICH MAY OR MAY NOT SEE
THE LIGHT OF DAY. IF HE HAS ANYTHING TO
SAY ABOUT IT HE'LL MAKE SURE IT DOESN'T
SUCK ASS.

AT LEAST HOLLYWOOD MOOKS DON'T GET
TO MOLEST THE COMICS, OF WHICH, ED
PREDICTS THERE WILL BE A MINIMUM OF 6
BOOKS IN THE HIP HOP FAMILY TREE
SERIES.

EMAIL: WIMPYRUTHERFORD@GMAIL.COM
TWITTER: @EDPISKOR
ADDRESS: YOUR MOM'S BEDROOM
WEBSITE: WWW.EDPISKOR.COM

THE ORIGINAL ART IS AVAILABLE BUT KEEP IN
MIND YOU'RE COMPETING FOR PURCHASE
WITH FAMOUS RAPPERS.

PHOTO BY GARRET JONES, USED WITH PERMISSION

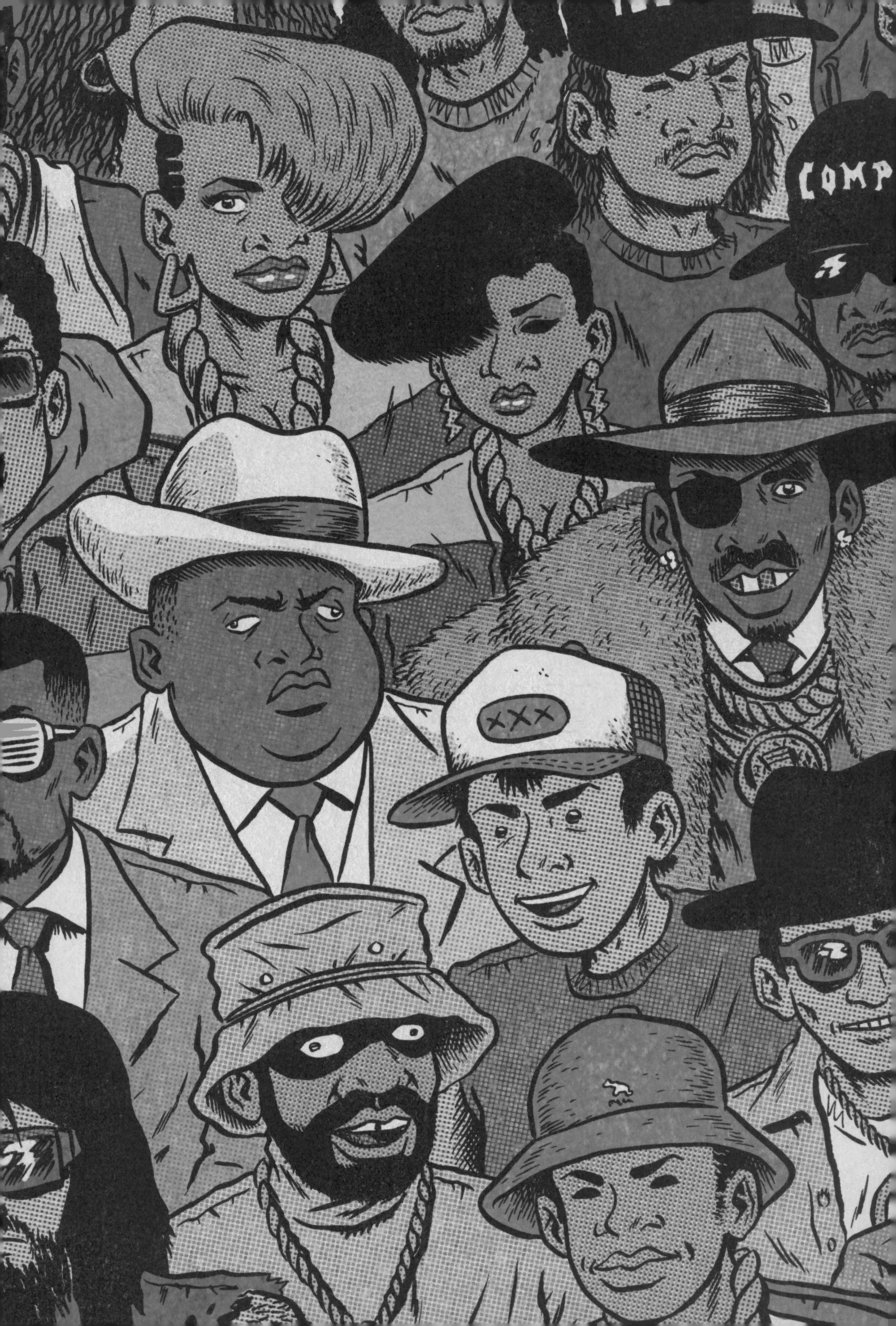
COMP
XXX